HOW TO BE A
SUCCESSFUL
SOFTWARE PROJECT
MANAGER

HOW TO BE A
SUCCESSFUL
SOFTWARE PROJECT
MANAGER

DR. TUHIN CHATTOPADHYAY

PARTRIDGE
A Penguin Random House Company

Print information available on the last page.

To order additional copies of this book, contact
Partridge India
000 800 10062 62
orders.india@partridgepublishing.com

www.partridgepublishing.com/india

Contents

Foreword

Digitization has become an essential ingredient for business excellence and software development lies at the core of digitization. Since last fifty years software project management framework has become stronger and more scientific. Software project management covers all the aspects of project including technical, functional and people oriented tasks. Still a high failure rate of software projects has been reflected by surveys and research work. All the software development firms and researchers are in the quest of a formula to optimize success of the software project. This book is an attempt to reach to a research based answer for the same. The major highlights of the book being the importance and transition of software development process from personal art of the developer to an application of scientific and metric based project management framework in the development process. Apart from this the new perspective of the software development process laid strong emphasis on the people factor in the project. The project brings together people with different skill set to achieve a common goal, and most of the teams in the project get dissolved after the closure of the project. This attribute of project makes it complex and tricky for team to work as a single unit. Understand the team dynamics at team and individual level help in achieving good results. The project managers will be able to understand the important factor for achieving higher success rate in the project through learning the need of people skill. Like all the other products, software development need to be highly customer oriented. This book throws light on management of all the project stake holders with a special emphasis on delighting the customer. The definition of software project success goes beyond its basic trio i.e. conformance to budget, time and functionality. Precise estimation, managing project baseline, developing and maintaining good quality software helps in enhancing customer satisfaction. The book also points out common mistakes done by the developers and project managers thus making project handling easy for them. I am sure that along with the project management researchers, the IT managers in the corporate too will find the book handy in managing the software development projects.

To

The Divine Trio…

Sri Ramakrishna, Maa Sarada and Swami Vivekananada

Chapter 1

Introduction

Today's corporate organizations have transformed into a new model of working which is more human oriented and not just focused of task management. The project is the current way of achieving efficiently the desired output. This model does not continue with the divided system of labor as in past. The discipline of project can be adapted to any business or industry due to its versatile, flexible and adaptive nature. The human centric, structured yet flexible approach and efficiency in output leads to the popularity of this approach.

The use of primitive form of project management can be traced down to as early as 2570 BC, during construction of Great Pyramid of Giza. One of the seven wonders of world, The Great Wall of China, 208 BC, had also been a large project. Although software engineering methods helped in developing quality software with scientific approach, it was not able to guide in terms of project management. Automobiles allowed effective resource allocation and mobility. Telecommunication system increased the speed of communication. The project was initiated by U.S. Navy in late 1956, and successfully launched its first Polaris missile in 1961. The historical journey of internet started from use of Advanced Research Project Agency Network (ARPANET) started in 1969.

The software industry grew rapidly In the 1970s and 1980s, as computer companies quickly recognized the relatively low cost of software production compared to hardware production. To manage new development efforts, companies applied the established project management methods. Cultivation of motivated and highly skilled software people has always been important for software organizations. The "people-factor" is so important that it has lead to the development of People Management Capability Maturity Model (PM-CMM). Software acts as a product and hence before a project is planned it's extremely important to establish the scope and objective of the product. This also takes care of the various tasks and their milestones. Finally the project aspect helps in planned and controlled software development. Like other projects the software projects also follow the set of management activities: Initiation, Planning, Organizing, Staffing, Directing, Controlling and Closure.

Figure1
Software Project Process

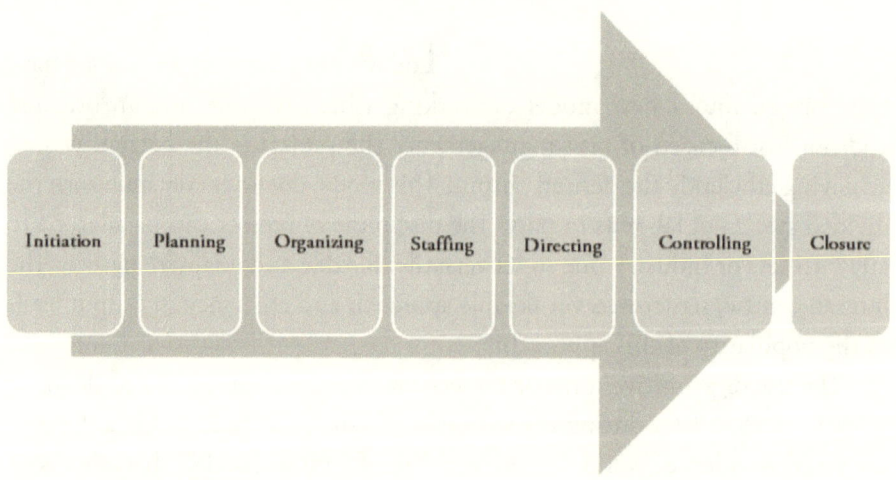

The Indian IT industry

In this digital economy, where organizations heavily relay on the use of information technology and information system, the importance of software and its development process is highly significant. Due to globalization and finding efficient and cheap and efficient resources a huge amount of work has been outsourced to Indian companies. The growth in the service sector in India has been led by the IT–ITES sector, contributing substantially to increase in GDP, employment, and exports. The major players in IT service industry in India are Tata Consultancy Services (TCS), Infosys Ltd, Wipro Ltd, Mahindra Satyam, etc. This conglomerate was the first one to have US$10 billion revenue in Indian technology companies (Mekikian and Roberts, 2009). The largest segment of the India IT services market is infrastructure services which were estimated at US$2.6 billion in 2008. In terms of market share, IBM has the largest market share in the Indian IT services market followed by Wipro and TCS-CMC. It has also been observed that there has been a drop in the average length of outsourcing contract from the accepted five years to three years specifically in infrastructure management segment. It has contributed immensely to the development of Indian economy. Information Technology has tremendous potential for the future of India. This will help India achieve faster, sustainable and more inclusive growth.

Knowing the critical success factors

Software project management is playing important role since late 1960s in achieving successful development of software. Development of software has always been a tricky process as it is both science and art. Also as compared to other engineering projects it is more complex and non consistent, where the nature of end product is intangible. Same applies to the software project management. Digitization is a matter of survival for today's business scenario. And so is the development of an effective, real time and cost effective digital solution. But on an average the software's that are developed are not able to satisfy above criterion. According to Mike Wooldridge (2000), President and CEO, *Micro Solutions,* good project management cannot guarantee success, but poor management on significant projects always leads to failure. High failure rates are being reported by many researchers inspite of the application of project management techniques (Mc Manus & Wood-Harper, 2008; Prinzo 2011; Riley, 2006). As per (Saur & Cuthbertson, 2003) a survey in UK showed that there were sixteen percent successful projects, seventy four percent challenged projects and ten percent were abandoned projects. With the increased importance of cross functional software packages, Enterprise Resource Planning (ERP) projects have also to be studied, for making their implementation successful. The failure rate of software is a major concern for the professionals even after decades of the application of software project management principles. The KPMG Canada Survey (2010) showed that in seventy percent organizations at least one project failed in a year. The failure of project is associated with huge cost overhead. Average budget per project of major federal Information Technology (IT) projects were more than double the estimated value during 2004-2009; it increased from $42 million in 2004 to $87 million in 2009 (Krigsman, 2010). And therefore it is not only important but interesting to understand and establish various factors that make a software project successful. Every project that have been completed or is undergoing give us insight into understanding what goes into making software project management a successful event. Lot of research and survey has also been conducted in this field, to understand this. Every work gives some idea into executing a successful project. So it is important to unleash the factors that make a software project successful. The list of success factor includes:

1. Requirement / Feasibility analysis
2. Team member's quality
3. Project managers' Quality
4. Project planning and process
5. Communication among stakeholders
6. Technical best practices
7. Testing
8. Client/ User satisfaction
9. Use of Automated tools in managing software projects

Further chapters focus on understanding and establishing the importance of these above mentioned factors and their relative impact on the success of the software project.

Chapter 2

Overview of Software Project Life Cycle

Project management provides a guideline to carry out any project in best way. As products have life cycle so does the projects and to understand it is important for better software development. Like other projects the software projects also follow the set of management activities: Initiation, Planning, Organizing, Staffing, Directing, Controlling and Closure. The order and importance of each step or phase is extremely important.

Initiation of the Project

Even before the planning is done a software project must be initiated. Basically development of any software (automation) is driven by some business problem. The software provides the solution to these problems, for e.g. if any firm is expanding and wants to have data of all the branches at headquarter through the internet based database application this can be achieved, which would be unmanageable otherwise. Thus identifying the problem and the need for automating any manual process is what initiates a software project. Once this is identified, a document containing the outline of the situation is prepared. This is followed by preparation of project feasibility report. This is required to save on the time and resources in case any project idea is not practically viable or does not serve the purpose. After establishing the feasibility and approval of the project the project manager and team are assigned to the project and the project scope statement is prepared.

Planning the Project

The next phase is of project planning. It is one of the most important phases of the software project life cycle as successful execution of the project depends upon perfect planning of the project. Project planning involves working out the details of the work required, estimating the time and cost to complete the project, to identify the resources competent to perform the task and highlighting areas of risk together with devising suitable contingency plans. It is also important because through planning it become clear what exactly has to done in the project and how to carry out the same. It consists of various sub plans: Software development plan, Quality assurance plan, Validation plan, Configuration management plan, Staff development plan, Risk management plan, Testing Phase and Maintenance plan.

Organizing the Project

After creating the document of the software project plan, the project manager needs to organize the software project in terms of manpower and other resources. The software development team generally follows a hierarchical structure; with the account manager and program manager at the strategic level and the project manager with his team at the execution level. Not only the team but the recourses in terms infrastructure and money for carrying out the work defined in the software project plan. This phase also results in the creation of the structure for executing the plan.

Figure 2
Structure of software development project

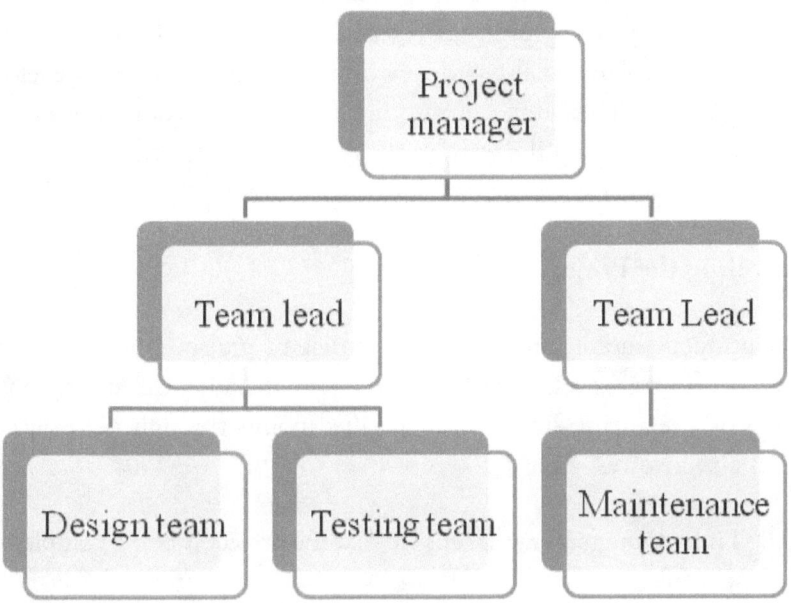

Staffing the Project

The software development projects require team of skilled professionals rather than a single person with a specific skill set. A group of people with different skill set work together as a team to complete the project. Hence it is essential to create the project team accordingly and if required people should be hired accordingly. Following activities are included in the staffing process:

i.   Recruitment and selection of the project resources with the right skills.
ii.   Orientation and familiarization of the new resource with the.
x.   Right training for the project work.
xi.   Equipped the project personnel with the right KSA and attitude.
xii. Performance appraisal of project resources by means of their contribution to the project.
xiii. Financial and non-financial remuneration in sync with the performance appraisal of the resources.

Directing the Project

Although this forms one of the phases of the project life cycle, in fact it is ongoing activity. The project manager takes care of implementation of the approved project plan and also performs other umbrella activities like selection of the right project resources, mentoring the project resources, supervising the resources, delegating the work to the resources, motivating the resources, meeting and coordinating with the resources.

Controlling the Project

Continuous monitoring and maintenance of project is required for the effective software development. Control also includes the definition and creation of a reporting structure at specified points through the project life cycle. It also involves:

i. **Time management**: To ensure that the project is being completed on schedule.
ii. **Cost management**: To check that expenses are assigned to right person and required.
iii. **Quality management**: To check whether the quality of the product or process is according to the specification or not.
iv. **Change management**: To determine change.
v. **Issue management**: To check issues.

Closure of the project

Sometimes this phase of the project is not given enough importance. As there are many stakeholders associated with the software project including the clients and the financial partners, it is important to wrap-up all the projects properly. Following must be kept in mind:

i. Writing a project closure report.
a. Redistributing resources that were assigned to the project
ii. Preparing any stepping stones for the next project.

Chapter 3

Requirements Analysis and Feasibility Test

A project has its own lifecycle which stage moves from the conception stage to the closure of the project. Project conception and initiation involves careful examination of the need to determine whether or not it benefits the organization. The third stage is launching/execution of project. Resources' tasks are distributed and teams are informed of responsibilities. The project performance evaluation and corresponding controlling measures is an ongoing process which is marked as the fourth stage and control. The digital era has lead to development of different types of software, used for both personal and business benefits. The very first step before developing any software is to understand the requirement of the users, find out the feasibility scope in terms of functionality and cost and finally defining the problem to be solved through digitization. The development of any software has its roots in some problem faced by an organization, for which it sought solution in digitization. Hence understanding the business need is a must. Any misjudgment and incorrect analysis of need leads to a failed project, as it does not meet the user's requirements.

The first step involves understanding the requirement of the user. Requirement analysis is critical for project success as it bridges the gap between the system requirement and system design. The broad objectives of requirement analysis are: to identify customer's needs, evaluate system for feasibility, perform economic and technical analysis, allocate functions to system elements, establish schedule & constraints and create system definitions. The most important aspect in requirement gathering is proper communication with the user. It is also important to take feedback from the user after the development of each prototype. Lack of communication and miscommunication leads to drastic failure rates. Once the requirement and need analysis is completed the project manager and the system analyst go for feasibility study. The economic feasibility, which involves cost-benefit analysis, is done. The technical feasibility is also evaluated to understand the resource requirement in terms of hardware, software and people. This is followed by legal feasibility and at the end alternative if any is stated and evaluated. At the end of this phase of the project the scope of the project is frozen. The benefits of feasibility analysis are:

1. The main aim of this step is to chalk out and describe the boundaries of the project clearly and finalize them by approval of the client. For this the evaluation of current situation is vital. A contractual agreement the organization and the client are done, for example preparing a statement of work. This helps in minimizing scope creep, as most of the client propose and demand incremental changes during the process and hence the scope of requirement changes. Hence understanding the need of the client clearly and freezing it with the proper documentation is essential for project success

2. The alternatives are to be evaluated both in terms of resources and the budget. Once the projects start changing plan in a very minor way bring huge cost and time overheads. The cash flow considerations are included in the scope definition and accordingly alternatives can be evaluated.

3. If feasibility analysis indicates that an idea has good potential, the software development firm can proceed with the project. Identification of associated risk, its quantification and mitigation plan can be done as a result of this analysis. It also helps in deciding whether or not the project should proceed for implementation.

4. At this stage ideas can be considered and tested in a safe environment, without much loss in terms of time, effort and cost.

5. The sponsors play an important role in influencing success of the project and supervising its governance. The sponsor's interest is importance also because they take accountability of business case and benefits, help in strategic decision making, critically reviewing progress of project and managing internal and external interfaces.

6. Help in identifying possible stakeholders. They can be: top management, project managers, team members, client, users and sponsors. Once the identification is done it becomes easier to manage them.

Although importance of requirement gathering and feasibility analysis is known to project managers and is also being practiced but still there are some complexities or shortcomings associated with this process that a project manager must take into account, in order to mitigate risks associated with the requirement and feasibility phase. In this regard there are certain points to be kept in mind:

a. At all phases of the software project new requirements can be expected from the client.

b. Very few applications are able to freeze upon eighty percent of the total requirement.

c. The system analyst must not include requirements that are not practically feasible.

d. Requirements regarding security of the application are generally not clear.

e. Lack of availability of standard, reusable requirements and designs.

f. Handling legacy data and application is a tricky job.

g. The documentation regarding the requirement and feasibly may be too large to prepare and implement while designing and coding.

Business Analysis

In the software project a system analyst plays an important role in finalizing the requirement and scope of the software application. But considering the extensive use of software's in all spheres of business analyst's role has also become very critical. Although as per the classical development model of software development life cycle (SDLC) business analysis activity is not part of development process, but it minimizes the gap of understanding between the business strata and the technical strata. Thus the step of business analysis is a primary step towards developing a better software application due to better clarity in the overall requirements.

Chapter 4

Team member's quality

Henry Ford observed "Coming together is a beginning. Keeping together is progress. Working together is success." The software engineering approach highlights the importance of four P's: Process, Project, Product and People. Initially when project management concepts were implemented, various industries including software development, focused mainly on proper planning and efficient distribution of task for good results. Gradually with experience and through surveys the organization started giving importance to people related factor. The project brings together people with different skill set to achieve a common goal, and most of the teams in the project get dissolved after the closure of the project. This attribute of project makes it complex and tricky for team to work as a single unit. Due to globalization the teams have becomes virtual in nature and hence the challenges of working in a team because of diverse team and online interaction causes adverse affect on team performance. Understand the team dynamics at team and individual level help in achieving good results.

The planning for building a fine team begins right from the recruiting appropriately skilled human resource. The first activity for this is making a proper plan for human resource required for the project. This helps in suitably defining the staffing, managing, controlling and release of a resource. After this the project manager or the project management team in collaboration with the recruitment cell must select the best people suitable for the project. In case of inappropriate selection, the project suffers due to discrepancies in the schedule, budget and quality of the project which leads to dissatisfaction of the customers. All these considerations apply to virtual teams as well. As discussed due to globalization and outsourcing of software development projects, the team interacts mostly online. The culture of work from home has also raised the popularity of virtual team. There is diversity among the members due to geography, time zone, culture etc. which hampers working as a single team. Transparent and clear communication is a major challenge in project teams, which further lead issues like, lack of trust, team conflict and inability to make proper decisions within time. Another thing which along with providing benefits bring along the challenges is, agile methods. Agile method is gaining popularity, and many software development organizations are shifting from traditional method to agile. The agile method upholds adaptive and people focused approach, with a small and collaborative team working closely. The team size factor is another people factor which effect project success. In order to maximize the chances of project success, certain factors related to team must be kept in mind. The chapter further discusses following team related factors:

1. Communication & coordination in team
2. Conflict management in team
3. Diversity in team due to space, time and geography
4. Trust
5. Motivation
6. Skill of team members & training
7. Job satisfaction & personal satisfaction
8. Empowerment and engagement of team members
9. Lack of shared vision

1. Communication & coordination in team

The effectiveness of team is highly hampered due lack of communication. Sometimes the team members are reluctant to communicate during the formative phase of the project team or often they are unaware of the communication channels to use within the team. Miscommunication not only create problem in carries out various tasks by the team but also pose problem in achieving common goals. This kind of situation also leads to duplication of work. According to survey done by psychologist OPP, on 2002 employees, 46% employees quoted poor communication as the reason for poor performance of the team. 24% employees blamed lack of clarity about the ultimate goal as the reason.

2. Conflict management in team

Conflict is inevitable when project team members interact for completing their tasks and responsibilities. Brain storming is essential for quality work but difference of opinion may lead to conflict within the team members. Two conflict management styles, confronting and give and take have beneficial effects on success of the project. Some possible underlying reasons for conflict among team members are:

- Resourcing issues and disagreements
- Arguments regarding equipment, specific facilities or software selections
- General costs and project expenditures
- Technical and design disagreements
- Differences of opinion on prioritization
- Lack of consensus on unified process methodologies
- Disagreements on the schedule or timeline
- Lack of agreement on key responsibilities
- General personality clashes and arguments

3. Diversity in team due to space, time and culture

The effect of some cultural factors on communication and productivity vary from culture to culture. Most of the project managers fail to understand the criticality of time zone and face problems in scheduling meetings across multiple time zones. When working with multicultural teams it is important to understand the basics of each culture. Accents also make understanding verbal communication a challenge.

4. Trust

Trust is acknowledged as one of the most important factor for the effective functioning of teams and organizations have realized this. This factor is also important for software development team. Trust within the team members leads to team satisfaction and relationship commitment, and help in lowering stress. In a trustworthy environment the members show affective commitment. Trust comes from faith and belief on coworkers, which is built over time. The temporary and often virtual nature of software project teams makes it difficult to do so.

5. Motivation

Team based approach for software development is beneficial because it helps in solving problems related to multi-dimensional and multi-discipline nature of work. This approach encourages you as staff with complementary skills and competencies, to coordinate your efforts. Motivation inspires, encourage and stimulate the work force to perform better. Motivation can solve the team performance issue in three folds, by handling the resistance for change, by helping team members in not getting distracted and be focused on the ultimate goal of the project and raising confidence of team members when dealing with novel tasks. The personal aims of team members also act as motivating factor. If the member is able to see a parallel between the organization/ project goal and his personal goal, the sense of motivation automatically comes, it is the project manager's task to identify this.

6. Skill of team members & training

Personnel, technical and functional capabilities of the team members is significantly associated with lower number of defects and enhanced productivity in packaged software products. Also, teams with higher experience in specific application domain of the product exhibit lower number of defects and thus incur lower maintenance costs. The problem for optimal team formation is an important issue for many software organizations especially for global virtual teams. These things should be kept in mind when the acquisition of the project team is done. If the team does not poses certain skill, then after proper training need analysis appropriate training should be provided to them. Organizational decisions regarding hiring, appropriately staffing and training project teams for high-performance must be made to ensure a team's success.

7. Job satisfaction & personal satisfaction

Employees with a predominant technical career orientation have more job satisfaction than those with a predominant managerial orientation. Retaining information technology employees has been a problem for software development organization as it is difficult to manage ramifications owing to attrition of the software professional. The global virtual nature of teams further enhances dissatisfaction as there is less face to face interaction. Job satisfaction has strong effect on productivity and performance. Job satisfaction is a multidimensional concept including satisfaction with supervisor, the work, pay, working conditions, appraisal, promotion. Organizations get benefitted by the presence of humanitarian values and indicate satisfaction at various levels of organization. As earlier discussed poor communication leads to ambiguity which have a negative impact on job satisfaction. The use of agile methods helps in developing higher job satisfaction among information technology professionals. Agile methodology follows human-centric bodies of practices and guidelines for building software in unpredictable and highly-volatile environments.

8. Empowerment and engagement of team members

Employee empowerment has been defined in many ways but generally means the process of allowing employees to have input and control over their work, and the ability to openly share suggestions and ideas about their work and the organization as a whole. Empowerment has expanded upon the concept of participative management. Involving team members in the decision making, by the manager is recommended for project success. Mallak and Kurstedt (1996) gave the model of empowerment which includes four concepts: intrinsically motivated behavior leading to, internal justification for actions taken whereby, management releases some of its authority and responsibility to other levels in the organization that deal directly with the product or, service integrating coworkers for problem solving. Multi dimensional nature of employee empowerment was highlighted by Honold (1997). In the multidimensional approach both the leadership component and the individual component will have an impact but individually they will not be able to explain project success. The multi-dimensional constructs given by them is:

- Teams and collaborative working arrangements.
- Decentralized structure of the organization.
- Contingent reward system.

Establishing an environment when employees feel free to question, challenge and offer new ideas can help to avoid this problem and benefit employees and leaders. Engaged people employ and express themselves physically, cognitively and emotionally as they perform their roles. The notion of flow (Csikzentmihalyi, 1975) is also related to employee engagement. Flow is the state in which there is little distinction between self and environment. When individuals are in the state of flow, they need little conscious control for their actions.

9. Shared vision

With the software project teams spread across various locations, the vision of the larger picture in terms of customer requirements and project objectives should also need to be shared.

Chapter 5

Project managers' Quality

The last chapter discussed the importance of people dimension and in specific the role of team in the success of the project. Project team efficiency is result of team effort under the guidance of project manager. Most of the team member are technical workers like developers, analysts, testers, graphic designers, and technical writers, possessing qualities like creativity and productivity and thus perform well. Inspite of this they require proper guidance and a direction which make them work as per the big picture in the project. The project manager is also required to provide clarity about role of individuals in the team while managing the expectations of senior executives and the team members. A project manager plays a pivotal role in a software project, being involved right from the planning and definition of the scope to the closure of the project. Apart from managing the project a project manager must also exhibit appropriate leadership quality. Following qualities of project manager in diverse roles leads to successful implementation of a software project:

1. Good communication with the Stakeholders

The very first step of any development process starts with defining the scope and understanding the feasibility of the project. The project manager plays an important role at this stage as he is the one who bridges the gap between the business and technical dimensions of the project. This helps is establishing clear requirements and specification as per the need of the client. Identifying various stake holders apart from the client is important for a project manager. Strong communication skills are critical to keep all stakeholders informed, supportive, and enthusiastic. A good rapport build with the client at this phase helps in eliminating lot of changes at a later stage. It is strongly recommended that client should be involved right from the initial phases of project, as it leads to better requirement quality and also act as a source of information for further improvement (Kujala, 2005). The business is brought by top management, but the project manager must establish clear communication with them so as to understand the ultimate vision of the organization. Top management support has high impact on project success (Zwikael, 2008). Apart from this including these third parties during project review meetings can help avoid sending inaccurate messages to the public.

2. Planning and organizing

"Plans are worthless, but planning is invaluable." said Peter Ducker. A project management comprises five processes which are initiation, planning, executing, monitoring & controlling and closing. A good plan provides the following benefits: -

a. Clearly documented project milestones and deliverables
b. A valid and realistic time-scale
c. Accurate cost estimates
d. Details resource requirements
e. Acts as an early warning system, providing visibility of task slippage
f. Keeps the project team aware of project progress

3. Resource handling

Project managers play an important role in effective monitoring and balance of recourse and their workload in a project or across multiple projects. They are require to go through the profiles of resources to understand their skills, interests, experience, language expertise, work preferences, availability and accordingly assign them to the project. With the global virtual teams in the project this work becomes all the more critical.

4. Managing, leading and bonding with the team

In contrast to the typical engineers, software is developed by teams of individuals who engage in creative problem solving. Teams are necessary because it would take too much time for one person to develop a modern software system. It's important for a project manager to effectively manage and motivate the team members. A manager's people skills are essential for achieving the ultimate business goal. Technical proficiency without leadership skill has undesirable project results. It is important to built rapport with the team members. These skills help project managers in exercising influence and authority to direct the team for working towards the ultimate goal and also enable them to act as bridge between business need and results of technical team. The conflict may arise due to diverse background skills, culture and values. According to PMBOK and Gobeli, Koenig & Bechinger (1998) conflict management styles—confronting and give and take—have beneficial effects on success at the organization level for the firms in this study.

5. Indentifying and providing training

Coach and train project team members on Software Development processes and best practices. Although the identification and recruitment of human resource is done very carefully, there may be certain technical and behavioral skills of the team members which may be required to enhance as per the requirement of the project. Project manager must effectively identify various training needs at individual and team levels to ensure the good results in the project. During the phases where software business undergo cost cutting training is considered as overhead, but a manger must realize that untrained or poorly trained team will cost significantly more to support than well-trained workers. Training also leads to longer employee retention. A project manger must recommend technical and behavioral training for team members apart from this project management software and training should be introduced to support managers also specifically for larger or multi-year projects. A project manager must recognize individual effort and rewards for team success for motivation.

6. Risk management capability

The risk management practice, involves risk identification, analysis, prioritization, planning, mitigation, monitoring, and communication. The risk associated with software project can be classified as follows:

a. **Software requirement risk:**

The risk while gathering the requirement, which is the initial stage of project leads to unsuccessful project causing customer dissatisfaction. This risk might creep up because of lack of analysis for change of requirements, change extension of requirements, lack of report for requirement, poor definition of requirements, ambiguity of requirements, change of requirements, inadequate of requirements, impossible requirements and invalid requirements.

b. **Software cost risk:**

Exceeding the estimated budget of the project leads to unsuccessful project. Cost overhead may be caused due to lack of good estimation in project, unrealistic schedule, improper working of the hardware, human errors, lack of testing, lack of monitoring, complexity and huge size of architecture, extension of requirements change, personnel change, management change, technology change and business environment change.

c. **Software scheduling risk:**

Inadequate scheduling and planning leads to poor result in software project implementation. This happens when there is inadequate budget, change of requirements and extension of requirements, human errors, inadequate knowledge about tools and techniques, long-term training for personnel, lack of experience of manager, lack of skill and lack of good estimation in projects.

d. **Software quality risk:**

One of the key requirements of the customer is fully functional quality software. But due to inadequate documentation, lack of project standard, lack of design documentation, inadequate budget, human errors, unrealistic schedule, extension of requirements change, poor definition of requirements, lack of enough skill, lack of testing & good estimation in projects and inadequate knowledge about techniques, programming language, tools the risk is associated with the quality aspect.

7. Use of automated tools for project management

The planning, estimation, resource handling, monitoring etc. all these task in the project are time consuming and require accuracy. Automated software helps in managing flow and transparency of project information, provide process guidance and integrate various project tasks. A dashboard facility provide effective visualizations making monitoring and decision making fast. The team is able to deliver the project much faster with collaborative tools. Use of automated project management is highly beneficial for project success, and hence all project managers must optimum use of such tools.

8. Project Closure

Projects need to be completed at the scheduled time to avoid unplanned expenditure. With the consent of customer if the critical success factors have been met, the project delivered, tested, released then project manger must recommend customer to sign the project off.

Software project management has laid down framework for conducting project in efficient manner. The tools, techniques and technological advancement have made the development project work faster and in cost effective manner.

Inspite of all these good things if the project is not supervised by a manger who is business driven and at the same time is peoples person, a project will not show good results. It is extremely essential for a project manager to possess leadership quality and if not so he should be provided appropriate training for the same by the organization. The managers must realize that with globalization the his role become all the more challenging where empowering the team, developing trust within the team and overcoming various conflicts due to diversity in geography, time zone and culture is essential.

Chapter 6

Project planning and process efficiency

Software project management is a blend of technique and art and hence to make it successful proper and realistic planning is required. Project managers are responsible for creating the project plan and to update it on a regular basis. Project planning involves working out the details of the work required, estimating the time and cost to complete the project, to identify the resources competent to perform the task and highlighting areas of risk together with devising suitable contingency plans. The plan must account for the dynamic nature of software development in global environment and reflect present situation. In most projects there are a number of unanticipated challenges or events which may affect the timescales, costs and outcomes of the project. Good plans help the manager in dealing with problems associated with these challenges.

Accurate planning of a software project, including proper sequencing and integration of essential elements of development process is very important for project success (Wideman, 2002). It is extremely important to set and define milestones and identify task interdependencies (PMBOK, 2008). It is also important to be able to deliver new software development in a timely fashion without the risk of business delays due to business environment changes and continue in the use of best practices in software development, which is not possible without proper planning. Various aspects of software development that require planning are:

1. Software development plan

It is the central plan, which describes how the system will be developed. Developing a project plan is as important as properly designing code. This stage specifies the order of work to be carried out, resources and responsibilities. Work breakdown is prepared and the project is divided into activities, milestones, deliverables; dependencies between tasks etc. It is on the basis of the project plan, contracts are signed and careers made or broken. During planning it is important to keep in mind overestimation and underestimation of above activities.

2. Quality assurance plan

It specifies the quality procedures & standards to be used. Software quality assurance plan is a must in order to set out standards to be maintained during project development. Standards related to documentation, coding and testing should be framed properly. The methods by which this is accomplished are varied and include ensuring conformance to one or more standards, such as ISO 9000 or a model such as CMMI.

3. Validation plan

This defines how a client will validate the system that has been developed. This involves checking of the software against its specifications. The details involve checking for requirement specification, checking each software item before it is used as an input to another and to check the validity for operational use. The main aim of software verification and validation is to trim down software errors to an acceptable level and may require a substantial effort of the total project resources, depending upon the criticality and complexity of the software.

4. Configuration management plan

It defines how the system will be configured and installed. This activity helps in minimizing the impact of any change on overall system. Proper planning in this area facilitates continuity of software development inspite of changes without incurring much overhead in terms of efforts, time and cost.

5. Staff development plan

This plan describes how the skills of the participants will be developed. Developing a project staffing plan involves selecting and assembling a project team. The staffing plan specifies when and how to meet the requirements for staffing the project. During recruitment the software organization, project sponsor and the project manager ensure that team members with appropriate experience and skills are selected but during the various phases of the project, members may need different technical and behavioral enhancement. This plan helps in describes in what way the skills and experience of the project team members will be developed. The important points to be considers while making this plan is to lay out and document the details for acquiring, the staff, specifying the duration for which the staff will be needed, the skills required to complete the project and set of training required by the existing staff. It's also essential to get commitments from key staff before actual work begins is necessary.

6. Risk management plan

While planning it's extremely important to know the key risks that a project can face. Accordingly risk mitigation and handling strategy has to be prepared. Normally a project manager should plan for staff turnover, management change, hardware unavailability, requirements change, specification delays, size underestimate, technology change and product competition. Planning for proper backup and recovery also help in handling risks.

7. Testing Phase

During this phase, the Software Test Plan (STP) will be developed. To deliver quality software to the customer through testing is essential and planning this process makes the testing more efficient. A document containing detailed plans and descriptions for various test cases is prepared. All the tests are performed as per the plan and the result are published and documented in the Software Test Report (STR). Preparing test plan helps in foreseeing the challenges ahead. It also serves as the means of communication with other members of the project team, testers, managers and stakeholders. Managing change easier by preparing this plan and by updating the plan at major milestone helps the manger to keep testing aligned with project needs.

8. Maintenance plan

Once the tested software is deployed at the users' site the project enters into maintenance phase. Unlike most of the engineering projects where maintenance of product is concerned with keeping the in working order and repairing it, the software maintenance phase is responsible for make necessary enhancement in the software to match the changing needs. The important point to note is that software products do not deteriorate with time, but they may fail to satisfy the functional requirement of the organization and the users. The software call for maintenance when the software models changes, new functionality is added and to run on improved hardware or with improved software. Basically the scope of this phase is corrective, adaptive, perfective and preventive. All this helps in fixing a fault in the software without changing or adding to the software's functionality, to preserve functionality in a changed environment, to improve software performance, maintainability, etc., and can extend the functionality of the application and to prevent further faults and to improve the structure and maintainability of the system.

The above mentioned aspects of planning are all required to fall in sync with the strategic planning. Software projects within program or portfolios are means of achieving organizational goal. While planning a project manager must keep in mind that the team members are clear about the overall vision of the organization and the goal of the project in specific. The factors resulting in the strategic organizational need and plan may result due to business need, customer request, technical advancement or legal requirements.

Figure 3
Demystifying Software Planning

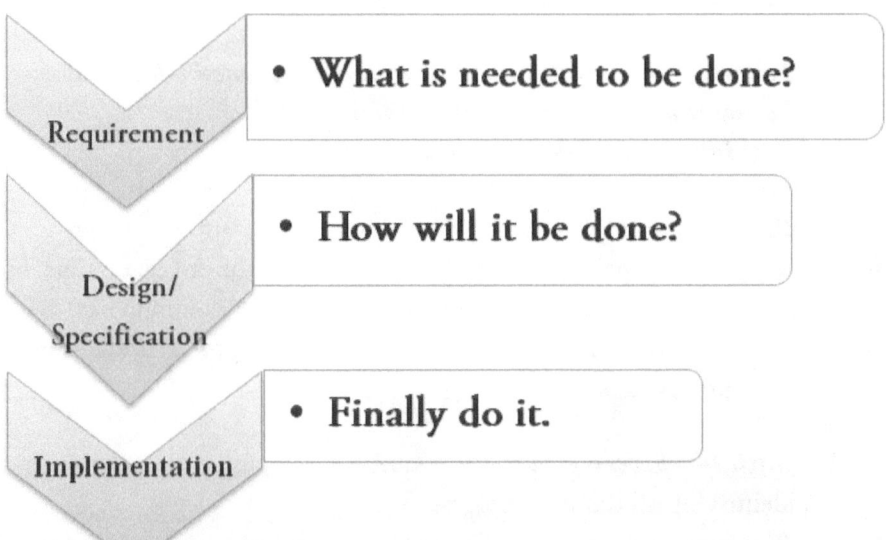

Process

Process is a set of interrelated activities performed to achieve a pre defined product, result or services. Planning is crucial to make all the tasks work as desired but in order to achieve success in a software project, it is essential to have efficient processes. Importance of software products in organizations and everyday life is continuously increasing and hence for development of quality software it is important to have predefined and efficient processes. The practice of regular assessment and improvement of the software development process, SIP (Software Process Improvement) need to be adopted in the software projects. The Capability Maturity Models (CMM) are an attempt to guide organizations to increase their software development capability and process maturity, the model suggests concrete measurements since the diversity of project environments may evoke varying measurement needs. The actual processes are compared against a set of "best practice" processes. It is important to right size the process to project needs. It is also important to adapt the development process to the appropriate lifecycle phase, to continuously improve the process, and to balance the project plans and associated estimates with the absolute uncertainty of a project, for this Agile development methodologies are suggested. The dynamic scenario of software development is supported by agile methods in following ways:

a. *Focusing on adaptive rather than predictive methodologies*
b. *Focusing on people rather than roles*
c. *Providing self-adaptive process.*

Insufficient planning is definitely a major reason for demise of IT projects. Without proper planning, the probability of completing the project on time, on budget or with the required functionality (which are three common factors for project success) is low. Following are the various process groups under project management process group

1. *Initiating process group*: This requires developing project charter and identifying all the stake holders.
2. *Planning process group*: Planning processes require development of project management plan, collect requirement, define scope, prepare WBS (Work Breakdown Structure), define activities, sequence activities, estimate activity resources, develop activity schedule, estimate cost, determine budget, plan quality, develop human resource plan, plan communication to all stakeholders, plan risk management, identify risks and plan procurement.
3. *Executing process group*: Execution process require project manager to direct and manage project execution, perform quality assurance, acquire project team, develop project team, manage project team, distribute information, manage stakeholders expectations and conduct procurement.
4. *Monitoring and controlling process group*: Project manager must monitor and control project work, perform integrated change control, verify scope, control scope, control schedule, control cost, perform quality control, report performance, monitor and control risks and administer procurement.
5. *Closing process group*: A perfect project call for proper closing of the project or phase, closing procurement, obtaining acceptance by the customer &sponsor and documenting lesson learned.

Project managers and higher management of software development firms must realize that efficient process eliminates most of the bugs and overheads. All such projects must go for CMM-based software process improvement (SPI) efforts. The initial step for this requires assessment of the current capability of the organization to develop software. After this process groups as mentioned above must be formed and team members must be given training for this. Making a development process efficient definitely make a software project successful.

Chapter 7

Communication with stakeholders

In building the understanding of software project success factors significance of stakeholder involvement has emerged recently. Cleland (1998) defined stake holder as individuals and organizations who are actively involved in the project, or whose interests may be positively or negatively affected as a result of project execution or successful project completion. A software project is declared failed when the end product i.e. the software, does not meet the requirements specified by the customers at the beginning or if there is cost and time overrun. Most of the time the non -conformance to the required functionality is due to lack of stakeholder involvement and poor stakeholder management. A good project manager realizes that involvement of stakeholders in the various phases of software development contribute in the quality software product. Identification and communication with all the stakeholders is critical for the software project. Following steps are required to do this in best way:

1. **Identification of stakeholders**
2. **Planning communication with stakeholders**
3. **Distribution of information**

4. **Managing stakeholders expectations**
5. **Reporting project performance**

1. Identification of stakeholders

Proper management of stakeholder requires listing all the stakeholders, so that managing and communicating with them can be planned effectively. All the people impacted by the project are involved and their interest in the project along with their impact on the project success is documented. It's important also to determine the influence of the stakeholders. Defining stakeholder's participation is the next step, which involves clarifying their role and participation, as not all stakeholders need to be involved in all aspects of the project in all life cycle phases.

2. Planning communication with stakeholders

The process of determining the information required by all the stakeholders and the ways in which it needs to be executed, is critical for project success. Inappropriate planning regarding this leads to troubles like delay in the urgent information, delivery of sensitive information to wrong audience and insufficient information. Project manager should do all the related planning in the early stages of the project, preferably during the development of project management plan. This helps in the suitable allocation of budget and time for the communication with stakeholders. Project manager must ensure that his valuable time is well utilized and he does not over allocate himself for long list stakeholder's communication and meetings. Regular review of the communication plan should be done, as it gives much better results in the project. Risk management is a critical activity of the software project management and it is important to plan for the risks associated with communication management plan. The risks associated with this phase may arise due to new set of information required by stake holders or in case when they are having conflicting requirements and expectations.

3. Distribution of Information

This requires making the relevant information available to different stakeholders as per the plan. The main task is to execute the prepared communication management plan and responding to the unexpected request for the new information. This can be well handled if during the planning stage the risks associated with communication management are foreseen by the project manager. Software project manager must carefully decide regarding sender-receiver model, choice of communication media, meeting management techniques and suitable presentation techniques. The outcome of this activity is a set of output for communication which includes, stakeholders notification, software project reports, project presentations, project records(electronic or physical), feedback from stakeholders and documentation of lesson learned during the project.

4. Managing Stakeholder's Expectations

In the current scenario the projects are dynamic and incorporating agile methodology is the way to achieve success, in the software project. With a set of advantages agile projects offer challenges in terms of changing expectations of various stakeholders. Actively managing stakeholder's expectations in this scenario definitely enhances the probability of project success. Unresolved issues related to stakeholder requirement increases the project risk which causes the disruption in the project progress. The pressure form stake holders generate risk and it is the responsibility of the project manager to identify the risk and process or the product and with respect to this their expectations may change during the project. Even managing the perception of the stakeholder is to be handled by the project manager.

5. Reporting Project Performance

The document of progress and performance of project is required in the reports. This is an ongoing process of comparing the baseline data with the actual data and hence communicating the progress of project along with the forecast of the project result to the stakeholder. The format varies from simple status information to an elaborate report depending upon the need of the stakeholder. With the use of automated tools in software project management dashboard status report has become easy. This facilitates percentage of completion, scope, scope, cost and quality. Elaborate reports also give information like analysis of past performance, current status of risk and issues, work completed during a given period, next set of tasks and summary of changes requested by the customer and approved in the current period. A report is considered complete only when it reflects the forecast of the completed project specifying time and cost.

Best Practices in Managing Communication with Stakeholder

Although software project management work provides the steps of communicating with stakeholders, to ensure best results there are few important things which a project manager must keep in mind for example he must establish good personal relationships with them as expertise alone does not inspire trust and credibility (McManus & Wood-Harper). Trust can be implanted only by keeping entire work transparent. Transparency improves productivity and accountability. The project reports give the status of the project and brings transparency but using the recommendations of stakeholders or established formal methodologies to support the project is required to enhance the outcome of the project. All parties involved on the project will achieve a better result if they work together hence treating them as partners is important. Use of collaborative technology for information dissemination and effective stakeholder engagement are a must in the current global era.

Responsibilities of Stakeholders

There is lot that stakeholder expects from the software project manager, and they exercise their rights in terms of obtaining information and project status reports. None the less there are responsibilities associated with these rights. At the initial level they must provide funding to the project. The strategic partners must educate developers about their business, to achieve final old goal. They should involve themselves in establishing clear requirements precisely and guide the project manager in prioritizing them. They must review and provide timely feedback regarding relevant work artifacts of developers and promptly communicate changes to requirements, if any.

Stakeholder's participation plays an important role in software project success, for which the project manager must ensure effective communication with them. Stakeholder management practices developing within the software community represent a paradigm shift towards this inclusive empowerment approach. The current trend is towards stable relationships build upon stakeholder accountability.

Chapter 8

Technical best practices

Software development has an interesting angle to it; software development process leads to technological advancements and itself is technology driven. The success of a software project is dependent upon the right choice of technology, tools and methodology adopted to carry out the project. Technical best practices provide a guideline to get good results in the software development project. According to W. Curtis Preston Monday, expert in backup & recovery systems and owner of Truth in IT Inc., "a technique or methodology that, through experience and research, has proven to reliably lead to a desired result – and should be followed except when there is a valid business or technical reason for not doing so". Although to follow best practice in every aspect is recommended this chapter specifically focuses on technical best practices in software development projects.

1. To Select Appropriate Development Methodology

A methodology is a collection of procedures, techniques, tools and documentation aids which will help system developers in their efforts to implement a new information system. The choice of suitable software development methodology is critical for software project success. In many cases the failure is the result of either not using a methodology or using the wrong methodology. Different project have different requirements and hence same approach for every project is not advised. Initially the methodology to build hardware i.e. Code-and-Fix model, was used for software as well without understanding the vital difference between the two. Then with the software engineering use getting prominent waterfall, incremental and spiral mythologies, software development became more efficient. After this the need for real-time applications and need for user involvement/ feedback gave way to prototyping, clean-room and object oriented methodologies. The changing business needs and globalization have made these methodologies insufficient to give good results hence modern approaches called Agile have become more useful. These methodologies are categorized as heavy and light. Traditional or heavy methodologies comprises of waterfall, iterative, rapid action development characterized by a defined plan in the beginning of the process which is frozen at that point and development process is linear and predictive. On the other hand light weight methodologies are defined as the one with no frozen plan, but requires planning throughout the development process, highly test driven, and the development process is non-linear & adaptive. The Agile methods that appeared first are eXtreme Programming, Crystal methods, Adaptive Software Development, Scrum and Dynamic Systems Development Method where as Feature Driven Development, Lean Development, Open Source Software Development and others evolved afterwards. The most widely used methodologies based on the agile philosophy are XP and Scrum. They differ in particulars but share the iterative approach described above. Scrum for software development came out of the rapid prototyping community.

2. Software architecture and design

The importance of right architecture for the software development process has become widely recognized by the project managers. Bass, Clements, and Kazman (2003) define architecture as "The software architecture of a program or computing system is the structure or structures of the system, which comprise software elements, the externally visible properties of those elements, and the relationships among them. Architecture is concerned with the public side of interfaces; private details of elements—details having to do solely with internal implementation—are not architectural." The criterion to choose an appropriate architecture is: functional and non-functional requirements, defining the boundaries and interfaces of the system and aligning with the stakeholders.

The widely known and familiar designs are:

a. **Layered**: A layered system is organized hierarchically, each layer providing service to the layer above it and serving as a client to the layer below (Shaw and Garlan, 1996).
b. **Pipe-and-filter**: In a pipe and filter style each component has a set of inputs and a set of outputs (Ambriola & Tortora, 1993).
c. **Client-Server Architecture**: A computer network in which many clients send and receive service from host computer. The types of client server architecture are:

    i. Thin client
    ii. Thick client
    iii. Asynchronous
    iv. Synchronous
    v. N-tier client-server

d. **Peer-to-peer**: A peer to peer is created when two or more computer systems are connected and share resource, without going through a server.

3. Software Project Risk Analysis

Many software projects fail to deliver acceptable system within time and budget. Most of these failures could be avoided if project manager's asses and plan well to mitigate the risks associated with the software development projects. Risk management is a series of steps whose objectives are to identify, address, and eliminate software risk items before they become either threats to successful software operation or a major source of expensive rework (Boehm, 1989). The risks which are known due to past experience can be mitigated easily but the one which are not known requires major preparation. Broadly these risks are the one related to user, requirements, project complexity, planning & control, team and organizational environment. The key to successful risk management is to identify all risks known to a project manager and build time in for risks which are not known. To manage risk involved in software development following steps are important:

a. Assess risk probabilities and effects- After risks have been identified and enumerated, the next step is risk analysis. Through risk analysis, Itransform the risks that were identified into decision-making information.

b. Develop strategies to mitigate identified risks- Risk management plans should be developed, after prioritizing the identified risk factors.

c. Invoke a contingency plan- When the quantitative detriments cross the threshold, a contingency plan is invoked.

d. Communicate- Provide visibility and feedback data internal and external to your program on current and emerging risk activities

e. Recover from crisis- After crisis management the team members should be awarded to induce them.

Software risk management is an intimidating task, the project managers who implement the proven processes ensures the success of the software project. The nature of software projects creates many risks that must be managed thoroughly to avoid the common weakness of many projects. Formal risk management process is recommended to manage complex issues associated with software development projects. Project manager can choose to be reactive or proactive about these problems.

4. Use of software specialists

Software specialists are a must for developing quality software. The project manager while selecting the team should keep in mind the various tasks in the project that require specialist. The specialists are needed for Configuration control, cost estimating, customer liaison, customer support, Database administrator, data quality, decision support, development, domain knowledge, security, performance, function point, graphical user interface, human factor, integration, scrum for agile, metrics, management, project planning, quality assurance, testing and technical support. Both software development and software projects are complex, not to be handled by generalists.

5. Software Reusability

The study and application of this idea has spawned another engineering discipline, called domain engineering which essentially mean a comprehensive, iterative, life-cycle process that an organization uses to pursue strategic business objectives. This format is still untapped by the software community at large, but potentially very useful. The main advantages of reusability are higher quality products, less development time, higher scheduling accuracy and reliability. The reusability may be in the form of reusable architecture, reusable requirements, reusable source code (zero defects), reusable designs, reusable help information, reusable data, reusable training materials, reusable cost estimates, reusable screens, reusable project plans, reusable test plans, reusable test cases, reusable test scripts, reusable user document and reusable human interfaces.

6. Coding techniques and programming practices

Good programming and coding practices forms an important factor in the technical best practice. The wise choices regarding the programming language and approaches largely depends upon the skill and experience of the programmer. The software developers need to make decision regarding the appropriate programming language depending upon the need of the project. For instance financial applications involve a lot of calculations and hence java and C# are the better option. Media, Advertising, and Design essentially involve lot of creative work and are based on prototype methodology so Languages like Ruby, PHP and JavaScript are more suitable. Enterprise Applications and Operational Software are based upon approach of reusability. Such applications are massive and complex built on layered architectural design approaches so java and c# the top choices. Thus Scala, C++, Erlang and Python serve the purpose. Following steps make the coding process efficient:

a. Coding Standards and Code Reviews

A combination of manual as well as automated code reviews is recommended.

b. **Coding Techniques**

The most important things are giving appropriate names to the applications and functions. The idea is to reflect the purpose of the function and the names should be meaningful.

c. **Documentation**

The main aim of program documentation is to describe the design of the program. Documentation helps others on the team to understand your work. Documentation can help the programmer who is making the modifications understand the code.

7. Software benchmarks and baselines

Benchmarking facilitates better IT service, especially better service monitoring. Baselines makes project manager familiar with the operational behavior of each application/server, clearly document what is "normal" for a server and/or application, identifies types of problems that arise even when the server is behaving normally. Baselines makes project manager familiar with the operational behavior of each application/server, clearly document what is "normal" for a server and/or application, identifies types of problems that arise even when the server is behaving normally. Performance benchmarking of application is essential before software deployment. Testing alone is not sufficient for quality software, performance benchmarking is required to remove bottleneck in application and infrastructure. The performance testing is an ongoing process and goes parallel to all the phases of a project. Performance benchmarking is not a trivial exercise and hence project manager must plan well for it.

8. Configuration Control

Configuration management used in software development is also known as unified configuration management. The major operational aspects of configuration management are:

a. **Identification**: Identification describes the structure, the nature of its element, their identity and gives access to each item version.
b. **Control**: This step organizes versions and changes to system items while keeping the coherency on the complete system.
c. **Audit and review**: This helps in validating the completeness of the product, for this enumerating all the components of the software product is important.

SCM may also include specialized change management for packaged application suites for example, Oracle Applications for enterprise resource planning.

9. International Software Standards

Like all other sectors software projects are also not unaffected by globalization and hence following international standards in the development project is a must. The use of standards has many benefits for any software development company. It helps in improved management of software by being able to meet planned schedules and budgets. The certification obtained by the organization brings new customers. Due to this, partnerships and co-development, particularly in a global environment, are enhanced.

10. Terminating or Withdrawing Legacy Applications

Like all products software also face problem of obsolescence. The obsolescence of software could be due to functional, technological and logistical reasons. The legacy software also become obsolete and requires proper transformation or termination. It's an application in which a company has already spent significant time and money. Usually, legacy applications are database management systems running on mainframes or minicomputers.

An important feature of new software products is the ability to work with a company's legacy applications, or at least be able to import data from them.

11. Protecting Intellectual Property in Software

Unlike hardware software is an intangible product and hence intellectual property rights are at the foundation of the software industry. Each affords a different type of legal protection. Patents, copyrights and trade secrets can be used to protect the technology itself. Trademarks can protect the name of a software company, its products and taglines, and prevent competitors from using similar names. Trademarks protect software brands, but not the software or code.

Chapter 9

Quality assurance through Testing

Good quality of the product is a key to customer satisfaction and software products are no exception. Software failure is a major concern for the software development organizations. In the previous chapter the importance of involvement of the customer involvement in the requirement gathering phase has been emphasized, it is equally important for the testing phase. Software development organizations are focusing on process improvement and Total Quality Management (TQM) for enhanced software quality and productivity of the development firm. Quality has become one of the key to software success as well as the key market factor for high technology. Software quality comes from good testing plan and methodologies. Software development firms need to allocate appropriate budget. Software testing, can be define that as a process of executing a program with the goal of finding errors (Swebok, 2004).

Bugs in software

Enrichment of software quality is the main purpose of the testing activity, so testing phase focus on systematic detection of all categories of errors.

Errors associated with software development are known as bugs. Bugs can be categorized as compile time and run-time errors. The compile time errors occur when the source code does not comply with the syntax of the programming language used for the development. These bugs are easy to fix and incur low cost and most of the modern compliers completely help in the process. Run time errors occur due to the logical incorrectness of the code. This category of bug is difficult to fix and cost incurring. Although documentation plays an important role while writing a code in establishing the clarity of the context, most of the time logical errors are tricky to fix. Software testing help in validating and verifying a computer program, so that the final application conforms to the requirement of the customer and satisfies the needs of stakeholders.

Test case

During testing phase testing team uses test cases to discover information regarding errors. Different types of tests are created to get different category of information. In another definition given by According to Ron Patton (2001) "Test cases are the specific inputs that you'll try and the procedures that you'll follow when you test the software." Test cases are not only useful in finding defects but also helps in discovering more and more bugs present in the code. It prevents release of premature product, assists managers in making ship / no-ship decisions. By using test case cost of technical support can be minimized. Assessing quality not only becomes easy but also facilitates verification of correctness of the product thus enabling quality assurance. Project manager must hire experienced testing team, which is essential for writing effective cases.

Strategies for bug fixing

The traditional approach required the testing phase to start only after freezing the requirements and coding process, but the agile methodology for development emphasizes the testing process to be an on-going process. But in any case there should be a systematic plan for the same. The software testing is done at offline and online level. Syntax checking, dry run (walk through), lint and inspection constitutes offline mode of testing whereas online strategy consists of black box, grey box and white box testing.

Offline strategy:

a. **Syntax checking**: The rules and grammar of a language in which the software's source code has been written provides framework for this testing. The developers are responsible for conducting this type of testing, which can be performed manually or with the help of automated tools. A compiler helps in detecting and correcting the syntactical errors.

b. **Lint program**: In order to perform the detailed syntax checking lint program comes handy. Whereas a compiler concerns itself primarily with code generation, lint is completely devoted to checking the code for a myriad of possible defects. For UNIX based systems lint is a standard tool but for other platform it is required to be purchased separately.

c. **Inspection**: The above two testing are performed by the software developers, where as inspection is a formal procedure where a team of programmers read through, to clarify the purpose of the code. It's an extremely time consuming procedure which often leads to conflict within the team, but is often recommended for time critical applications involving safety.

d. **Dry run/ walk through**: The programmers try to mentally work out all possible outcomes of the code written. This form of testing is expensive in terms of time and human effort and sometimes impossible for large applications. Since this testing involves mental run of a program by scrutinizing the source code step by step to determine what it will do when actually run, can be used for discussion purpose. It provides a practice exercise and gives the outcome of all functionality on different values of input variables.

Online strategy:

a. **Black box testing**: Black box testing focus on the output requirements, without requiring the knowledge of internal structure of the program and code of the software. The main advantage of this method is the ability to perform optimum number of test cases, decreasing the effective time for testing.

b. **White box testing**: White box testing, also known as clear box testing and clear box analysis, unlike black box technique focus on the detail of the program. Thus the main advantage of this technique is the ability to check all independent paths in the entire module at least once. All logical decisions and iterations/options in loops are executed and tested.

c. **Grey box testing**: A comparatively new methodology of testing, gray box testing is applicable in the scenario where prior knowledge regarding the code and its logic is available to the software developers and testers.

Black box test styles:

i. **Function testing**: This category of testing focuses on testing of functions in component or system.

ii. **Domain testing**: Domain testing helps in identifying and removing domain errors, which essentially mean removal of error due to wrong execution of the program on certain specific input.

iii. **Specification-based testing**: This testing is also referred as behavioral testing. It broadly emphasizes the conformance of the user requirement in terms of system specification. The testers have no knowledge of how the system or component is structured inside the box.

iv. **Risk-based testing**: This test is performed to check the lack of quality as revealed by defects. Advantageous in mitigating risks associated to the software development.

v. **Stress testing**: In stress testing emphasis is on robustness of the software. In this non functional testing ability to handle run time error under heavy load is checked.

vi. **Regression testing**: Users/customers often request change in the requirements during development phase and regression testing handles the errors caused due to these changes.

vii. **User testing**: Acceptability of software by the users is a major concern in software projects. The last phase of testing is done by the users and generally at the client's site. The conformance to the functionality agreed upon during requirement gathering phase is must for the successful project. This is also known as beta testing and the version of the program or the software is also known as beta version.

viii. **Scenario testing**: In order to ensure proper end to end functionality of a software, scenario testing is done. This helps in achieving efficient working of all the business process flows of the software. The testing is done by the testing team keeping in mind the real time scenarios from the point of view of the end users. In scenario testing, testers take assistance and feedback from clients, stakeholders and developers to create test scenarios.

ix. **State-model based testing**: State machine implementation-independent specification (model) of the dynamic behavior of the system state: abstract situation in the life cycle of a system entity (for instance, the contents of an object)

x. **High volume automated testing**: In high-volume automated testing, the test tool generates the tests, runs them, instead of the testing team writing the test case and performing the testing manually. This approach makes the testing process much faster and effective.

White box test types:

White box testing primarily includes Unit testing and Integration testing.

1. **Unit testing**: It is testing of individual software units or groups of related units, where a unit is a software component that cannot be subdivided into other components (IEEE, 1990). Unit testing ensures that correct and bug free code is available for code integration. Most of the developers are responsible for conducting unit testing (IEEE, 1990)

2. **Integration testing**: A next step to unit testing, Integration testing involve testing of software components, hardware components, or both are combined and tested to evaluate the interaction between them. Test cases are written for this which examines the interfaces between the various units (IEEE, 1990).

Unit Testing is further categorized as:

1. **Execution Testing:** To figure out whether the actual result is matching with the desired one.

2. **Operations Testing**: This is done to check whether the software works as per the customer's expectation in conjunction operating system like Windows Vista, Windows XP, Windows 7 etc.

3. **Mutation Testing:** This test is done to check the efficiency of test cases by intentionally introducing errors in the code.

Approaches in Integration Testing

There are two ways in which the modules of the software can be integrated, top down and bottom up.

a. **Top down Approach:** The entire task of software development is divided small modules, while these modules are under development the main module is tested using stub. A stub is a temporary program substituting for the modules under development.
b. **Bottom up Approach:** This approach focus on creating the software in terms of small modules and later on integrating them all to form the complete software product. After testing the modules are integrated.

Test Plan

A Software Test Plan is a document describing the testing scope and activities. It is the basis for formally testing any software/product in a project. The main testing plan is documented in master plan whereas the other smaller procedures for testing are termed as phase test plan. The master test plan is a single high-level test plan for a project/product that unifies all other test plans. The level specific plans are the previously mentioned one i.e. unit test plan, integration test plan, system test plan and acceptance test plan. A test plan template provided by IEEE standard is used for software test documentation. This template provides a summary of what a test plan can/should contain.

Automated testing

An automated testing procedure uses software tools for testing unlike the manual software testing, where high human involvement is required. With the help of automated tools it becomes possible for the testers to perform predefined testing actions, with less efforts and time. This also helps in comparing the expected behavior of the software against the actual one.

Agile Testing

Agile software development is based on the concept of aligning the development process, with the frequently changing needs of the customers. For this kind of development methodology the testing mode should also be in sync with the agile development. This strategy focuses on, accurate planning in the software testing and transparency with the customers. Thus agile testing means, the practice of testing software for bugs or performance issues within the context of an agile workflow. Extreme Programming is one of the most well known agile development methodology. Since Customers, developers and testers constantly interact with each other, so regular adaptation to changing circumstances is possible and even late changes in requirements are accommodated.

Figure 4
Software Testing Life Cycle

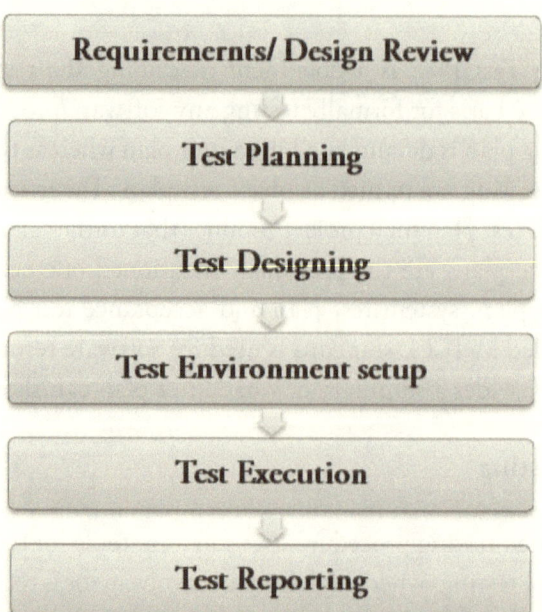

Quality of the software product has been a major concern for the software development firms. The technical aspects and the customer satisfaction are the key component to make a software project successful. Testing phase plays an important role in delivering quality bug free software. For better results apart from testing inspection, audit and agile testing is recommended. The quality of the software through testing is enhanced by both preventive and corrective approaches. In large projects and global projects involving geographically dispersed teams, both generalist and specialist should work in testing phase for better results. Through proper testing the number of bugs is minimized and hence the product is released in proper time, which brings down the cost overhead due to software project delay. The software development firms must Software organizations must perform cost benefit analysis' to determine how much to spend on testing.

Chapter 10

Customer Satisfaction through Better Pricing

Information Technology (IT) and Information Technology enabled Services (ITeS) has contributed a lot in the economy of India. According to NASSCOM (2009) annual revenue of IT based BPO was US$ 17.7 billion, inspite of this level of revenue generation; almost fifty percent of the outsourced IT projects have reported customer dissatisfaction (McEachern, 2005). It systems are acting as competitive advantage in all industries and at the same time poses risk if the software system fails.

The project success profoundly depends upon the satisfaction of the users and customers. Like all businesses the success of IT sector also needs to focus on enhancing customer satisfaction in the delivery of services and products. With respect to software products achieving satisfied customers is much more difficult, as it depends upon how effectively the development process delivers the final product as desired by the customers. Kotler has defined satisfaction as "a person's feeling of pleasure or disappointment resulting from comparing a products' perceived performance (or outcome) in relation to his or her expectations". It is ultimately the customer satisfaction through which any organization generates long term benefits. Apart from the reports of customer dissatisfaction one more thing that needs attention is the fact that during recession, for cost cutting the software firms reduce customer support. Reduction or withdrawal of customer support has adverse effect on customer satisfaction. To understand what factors in the software product and services makes a customer fully satisfied is critical for software project success.

According to Peter Drucker, "Quality in a service or product is not what you put into it. It is what the client or customer gets out of it." The satisfaction of the customer with respect to the software product can be linked to the basic definition of the software project success. The successful software project is the one which is completed within budget, time and delivering all the functionalities, achieving the business objectives. The project manager needs to focus on these factors to create more satisfied customer. Thus a deep understanding of ways to keep the project on track so that it complies with the definition of the software project is critical. There are two very important activities which help in doing so; estimation and developing baseline budget for project. For project managers it is very important that the cost estimation is being done very accurately, to make a software project successful. When a project fulfills all the promised functionality with estimated budget and time, customer is highly satisfied and a satisfied customer has enormous contribution in the success of the software project.

Estimation

Estimation helps in predicting the cost of resources required for a software development process. In order to estimate the cost following parameters need to be calculated:

1. Effort required to complete the activity- measured in man-day (person-day), man-week, man-month
2. Calendar time needed to complete an activity as per the allocated resources- measured in hour, day, week, month, year
3. Cost of an activity- total cost of an activity

Project estimation and project scheduling are carried out together for efficiency. And so the cost of effort is comprised of both the cost of estimation and cost of scheduling. Inspite of this certain initial estimates are required to be done by the project manager in order to project a rough estimate of the cost of the software to the customer. The major cost of a software project comes from the effort cost, but while deployment of the software at the customers site a large portion of the budget may be used up as traveling expense. As the current software projects in present era involve large number of virtual teams, the cost of travelling is reduced as communication is provided over internet based applications like e-mail, shared websites, shared drives, video conferencing and enterprise based social media. The effort cost not only includes the salaries of software developers but also the cost of running the software firm. These may include costs of providing, heating and lighting office space, costs of support staff such as accountants, administrators, system managers, cleaners and technicians, costs of networking and communications, costs of central facilities such as a library or recreational facilities, costs of employee benefits such as pensions and health insurance. There are various methods of software cost estimation. It helps in calculation of cost of various options minimizing the error. Apart from algorithmic estimates methods like expert judgment, estimation by analogy, Parkinson's Law, and pricing to win are also used. These methods may use either top down approach or bottom up approach. Top down approach suggests starting at the system level and assessing the overall system functionality and how this is delivered through sub-systems. On the other hand bottom up approach suggests starting at the component level and estimating the effort required for each component. Adding these efforts gives the final estimate. One of the myths of software development activity is that the time required completing a project proportional to the number of people working on the project.

Project Baseline

After the estimation an approved time phased plan must be prepared and published by the project manager. This helps in understanding the difference between the baseline set at a particular point and the actual progress of the project. But it's a big challenge for a project manager to decide about the baselines. A project is susceptible to change in requirement from the customer in between and these results in the scope creep. The scope is defined early in any software project during the planning and estimation phase, even minor change in the scope have high impact on schedule, cost, risk and quality of the software project. Thus it is extremely important for the project manager to effectively control and manage the project scope and minimize the scope creep. Hence the scope of the project must be defined clearly, communicated well to all the stakeholders and reconciliation of the emerging request must be handled by the project manager properly. The baseline budget is the tool used for measuring the affect of changing request on the planned schedule and budget for the success of the project. Ideally no project has a static scope, due to the changing customer needs and business environment; to accommodate change in scope new baselines are added to the software project. The baseline being a benchmark to measure performance against represents an understanding of the costs of the project based on the scope of the project. The initial baseline helps in preparing the budget, so that it can be approved by the company's financials. There may be situation in which the organization itself request for the re-estimation or re-baseline of all the projects for the corporate budgeting. It may be due to major gap identified in the estimates of some of the tasks. Such gaps must be communicated to the project sponsors. Proper documentation of all the changes is recommended and project progress must be reviewed regularly for effective results. Project management software comes handy in managing all this. Thus the scheduling, planning and incorporation of changes become easier and much manageable task. Apart from this the difference from the baseline is also minimized.

Software Product Quality

Software products unlike other products are intangible in nature and hence measuring the quality of the software is tricky. Software quality plays an important role in achieving customer satisfaction. For a software system sometimes it is difficult to achieve customer satisfaction as there may be conflict between the customer quality requirements (e.g. efficiency or reliability) and developer quality requirements (e.g. maintainability or reusability), this may also be due incomplete, inconsistent, or ambiguous software specifications. It is extremely important for a project manager to manage quality activities properly. In order to maintain the quality of software quality management activities must be carried out in the project very religiously. There are three major components of quality management activities:

1. **Quality assurance**
2. **Quality planning**
3. **Quality control**

1. Quality assurance

This helps in establishing organizational quality standards and procedures. These are umbrella activities applied throughout the software development process. Main elements of quality assurance are:

i. **Standards** – ensure that standards are adopted and followed.

ii. **Reviews and audits** – audits are reviews performed by SQA personnel to ensure that quality guidelines are followed for all software engineering work.

iii. **Testing** – ensure that testing id properly planned and conducted.

iv. **Error/defect collection and analysis** – collects and analyses error and defect data to better understand how errors are introduced and can be eliminated.

v. **Changes management** – ensures that adequate change management practices have been instituted.

vi. **Education** – takes lead in software process improvement and educational program.

vii. **Vendor management** – suggests specific quality practices vendor should follow and incorporates quality mandates in vendor contracts.

viii. **Security management** – ensures use of appropriate process and technology to achieve desired security level.

ix. **Safety** – responsible for assessing impact of software failure and initiating steps to reduce risk.

x. **Risk management** – ensures risk management activities are properly conducted and that contingency plans have been established.

2. Quality Planning

It is concerned with selection and modification of applicable quality standards and procedures for a particular project. During the planning phase a project manager also need to plan for the quality assurance and control. A software quality plan describes how an organization in general and project in specific will achieve its quality objectives. It describes the quality objectives and specifies the quality assurance and control activities to be performed in day-to-day company operations. In the case of a software development organization individual quality plans may be prepared for each software project.

3. Quality Control

Plays an important role in ensuring quality standards and procedures are followed by development team, it examines the software development process to ensure that all relevant procedures and standards are being followed. Quality Control (QC) ensures that the final product is error free and satisfactory. QC is also referred as testing activity. There are two basic approaches towards quality control: quality reviews and software measurement and assessment.

Figure 5
Software Quality Assurance (SQA)

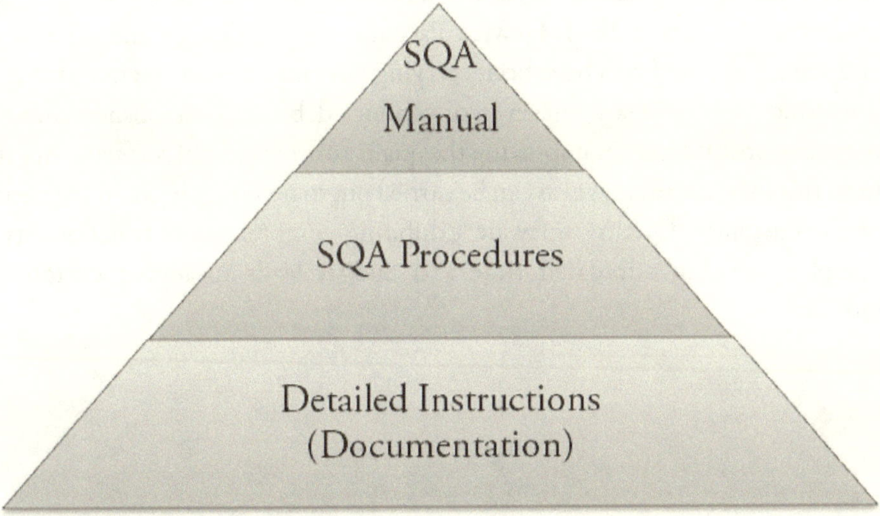

Customer Support and Service

Once the project is completed and the software product is ready it is important for the technical team to impart customer training. Giving user-friendly assistance for individuals having technical problems with software applications increases satisfaction level of the customer. When the project enters into maintenance lot of technical support is required by the client. The technical support team is composed of individuals that are familiar with the ins and outs of the software. With this knowledge, they are able to troubleshoot most problems that a user experiences.

Conclusion

In the field of software products customer satisfaction depends upon the evolution of software development project to create an operational software product. The product must satisfy the perceived and actual needs of the customer. During recession when most of the organizations focus on cost cutting sometimes quality of the product and support services are neglected, which have adverse affect on customer satisfaction. Project managers must plan and perform annual and semi-annual customer survey at organizational and project level. This helps in understanding the requirements of the customer in a better way. Use of automated quality control tools is recommended for better results. And in this global era lot of web based tools are available just to conduct quality related survey. IBM, Hewlett Packard, Unisys, Google and other big and small software firms have been carrying out customer satisfaction survey. This kind of benchmark surveys are conducted by well established survey organizations and help in improving the quality of commercial software. Apart from this in house surveys also can be carried out to better understand the need of the customer. Quality software exhibiting comprehensive functionality, completed within stipulated time and budget leads to higher customer satisfaction.

Chapter 11

Software project success through Automated Project Management

Lot of effort goes into making a software project successful; right from appropriate requirement gathering, studying the feasibility, planning effectively, managing the risk and proper maintenance of the software product. The nature of software projects have become multi dimensional, multi project and highly collaborative in nature, and hence the importance of automated planning for the software project must be appreciated by the project manger and the respective software development firm. It enables the team to plan and control the work. Centralized and continues progress of a project can be efficiently monitored. It also helps in forecasting trends and hence managing time constraints. It also requires coordinated approach. The solution is to use Project management software, which allows a more efficient management of projects. With increased access to project data, sound decisions can be made. Importance of automation in software project management is well established, and while selecting any automated tool a project manager must check for the following properties of the tool:

1. **Flow of information**
2. **Transparency in information flow**

3. **Process Guidance by the automated tool**
4. **Visualizations provided by the tool**
5. **Integration of information for decision making.**

The major benefits of the automated software project management tool can be categorized as:

1. **Project planning**: A project planned well eliminates most of the errors. The result of such planning results into:

   i. A detailed breakdown of tasks to be completed.
   ii. Task assignments, identifying who is responsible for which aspects of the project.
   iii. A time estimate for each task.
   iv. Links between dependent tasks.

2. **Task Management**: Ability to plan and allocate a task.
3. **Sharing and collaborating information and document**: With the ever increasing global virtual projects it becomes all the more important as they work with remote team members. DreamTeam, Central Desktop, GoPlan, ProjectDesk, and DotProject. Microsoft SharePoint and LiveOffice also offer these collaborative features.
4. **Sharing calendar and contact list**: While scheduling meeting with different members, that to globally dispersed these facilities save on time. Even for smaller work well shared spreadsheet also help in doing so.
5. **Managing issues and bugs**: For technical projects, this functionality is often used to track bugs. Technical problems requiring resolution of the issues and storage of lengthy descriptions, comments, each becomes much easier to handle using these tools. Thus both managing and handling of issues and bugs becomes more effective with the use of the automated tool. Some of the examples Jira, FogBugz, DoneDone, Unfuddle, and Kayako.
6. **Tracking time**: It is important to measure the time devoted by each team member for each task. With large number of member in the team and the one involving dispersed team this task becomes complicated.

7. **Ability to manage risk and forecast**: These tools also help in Knowing project risks, creating forecasts and tracking budgets.
8. **Reporting capabilities**: Keeping projects and tasks on schedule become manageable for a project manager, by providing flexible report formats and the ability to quickly access needed data
9. **Mange project costs**: Cost controlling as an important factor for project success. Project management software generally includes tools that can assist in managing project costs.

Following is the list of some of the popular software project management tools:

1. **Microsoft Project:** One of the oldest and user friendly tools is quite popular with the project management professionals.
2. **Basecamp:** To collaborate distantly located project resources.
3. **Central Desktop:** It's particularly strong in integrating with email-based workflows. It also has a free version that supports up to two workspaces and five users.

Chapter 12

Common mistakes in Software Project Management

The software project management frame work has been effectively laid down and the software development professionals are aware of the classical life cycle but still the commit some mistakes which put their effort in vain. The major categories under which these mistakes can occur are:

1. **People related**

    a. **Undermined motivation**: While supervising the complex tasks in the software development process and chasing the deadlines a project manger may tend to appreciate that for quality work all the members in the team whether technical or nontechnical need to be constantly motivated for quality results.

    b. **Weak personnel**: As choosing the right the right tool and technology is essential for quality software development similarly choosing personnel with appropriate skill and experience in vital for the software project success.

c. **Uncontrolled problem employees**: A successful project manager needs to be quick in identifying conflicts within the team and individual problems. After identification an appropriate solution for the issues must be found and applied.

d. **Adding people to a late project**: The myth that adding more people in the software development project when the deadline is approaching speed up everything needs to be demystified. It takes some time for people added in between to the project, to understand the work and start delivering.

e. **Friction between developers & customers**: Customer needs to be in touch with the development team right through the inception to the delivery of the software project. Frequent feedback from the customer help in delivering high quality software. The customers too need to cut down on their unrealistic expectations.

2. **Process related**

   a. **Overly optimistic schedules**: Before starting the project a project manager needs to estimate the stipulated time and cost for the software project. Most of the time managers end up giving too optimistic estimates. This leads to project failure and put the developers under high pressure which hampers their productivity.

   b. **Insufficient risk management**: While planning a project software project manager must take into account all the learning's from the past project as well plan for the unexpected problems.

   c. **Insufficient planning**: Efficient planning regarding schedule, budget, human resource and technology/ tools must be done by the project manager.

   d. **Omitting necessary tasks from estimates**: While estimation even the smallest task and resource must be counted to prepare realistic estimation.

3. **Product related**

   a. **Requirements gold-plating**: Certain requirements in a project may be task related not necessary from the beginning or right through the project. Such requirements must be handled with an optimal approach.

b. **Feature creep**: Most of the software projects are associated with the scope creep. It is extremely important to freeze the requirement at the beginning and gets it approved by the customer.

c. **Developer gold-plating**: Sometimes the developers are not aware of the ultimate business need of the software to be developed and they tend to apply incorrect tools and technology in the development process which have negative impact on the end result.

d. **Push-me, pull-me negotiation**: Managing and approving the correct schedule of all the tasks within the project is tricky but necessary for all the development projects.

4. **Technology related**

a. **Silver-bullet syndrome**: Choosing the appropriate development technology including the best language and the one that are proven effective for the similar projects is important.

b. **Overestimated savings from new tools or methods**: New technology and tools definitely improves the speed for the various tasks but if the framework in ineffective even this cannot provide major schedule jumps.

c. **Switching tools in the middle of a project**: As adding new people in the middle of the project in not very sensible similarly switching the new tools in the middle of the development process is not wise.

d. **Lack of automated source-code**: Automated source code help in effective coordination among the developers which is not possible manually.

Conclusion

Through automation of project management activities the error in terms of schedule and cost overrun can be minimized. This not only speedup the project but also help project manager in planning and executing the project efficiently. Apart from this use of formal project management methods exhibited less variability than use of formal decision-making methods.

Chapter 13

Result

The data are collected from one hundred and fifty software professionals across the leading IT organizations across India on the following ten variables:

1. Success of the project and
2. Clarity of understanding of requirement or feasibility analysis,
3. Team member's quality,
4. Project manager's quality,
5. Project planning and process efficiency,
6. Communication with stakeholders,
7. Technical best practices,
8. Testing,
9. Client/ user satisfaction and
10. Use of automated tools in managing software projects.

We have performed multiple linear regression keeping our dependent variable as the Success of the project and the remaining nine variables as the independent variables. To perform the linear regression, I need to first check the basic assumption of linear regression i.e. linearity. To find the linear relationship between the success of the project and understanding of requirement/ feasibility analysis Figure 6 has been drawn, which clearly shows that there exists a linear relationship between success of the project and clarity of understanding of requirement or Feasibility analysis.

Figure 6
Linear Relationship between success of the project and clarity of understanding of requirement or feasibility analysis of requirement

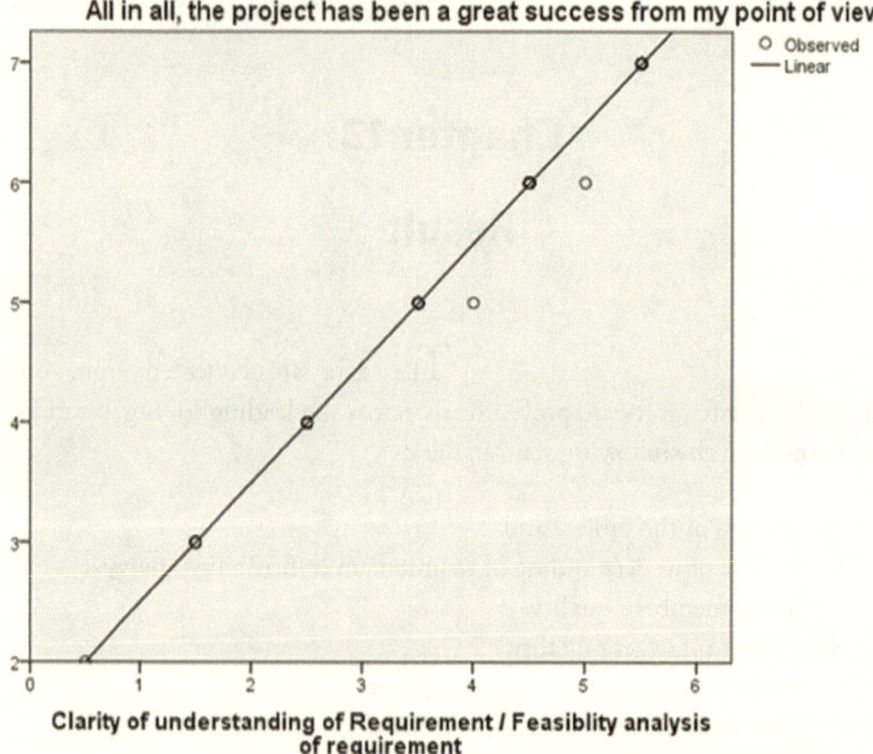

Clarity of understanding of Requirement / Feasiblity analysis
of requirement

To confirm the relationship between the success of the project and understanding of requirement or feasibility analysis a t-test have been performed and in the Table 1 shown below the p value is less than 0.05 therefore there exists a relationship between the success of the project and understanding of requirement or feasibility analysis.

Table 1

Linear Relationship between success of the project and clarity of understanding of requirement/ Feasibility analysis of requirement

	Unstandardized Coefficients		Standardized Coefficients	t	Sig.
	B	Std. Error	Beta		
Clarity of Understanding of Requirement or Feasibility Analysis of Requirement	.999	.005	.998	217.645	.000
(Constant)	1.499	.020		74.240	.000

To find the linear relationship between the success of the project and team member's quality Figure 7 has been drawn, which clearly shows that there exists a linear relationship between success of the project and team member's quality.

Figure 7
Linear relationship between success of the project and team member's quality

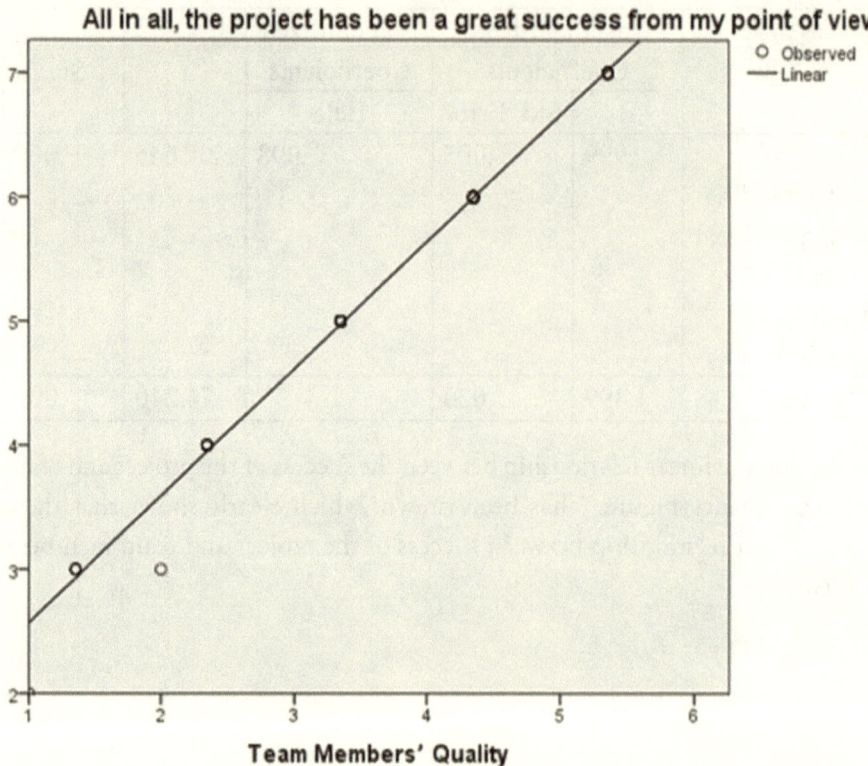

All in all, the project has been a great success from my point of view.

Team Members' Quality

To confirm the relationship between the success of the project and team member's quality a t-test have been performed and in the Table 2 shown below the p value is less than 0.05 therefore there exists a relationship between the success of the project and team member's quality.

Table 2
Linear relationship between success of the project and team member's quality

	Unstandardized Coefficients		Standardized Coefficients	t	Sig.
	B	Std. Error	Beta		
Team Members' Quality	1.023	.006	.998	175.615	.000
(Constant)	1.547	.025		62.497	.000

To find the linear relationship between the success of the project and project manager's quality Figure 8 has been drawn, which clearly shows that there exists a linear relationship between success of the project and project manager's quality.

Figure 8
Linear relationship between success of the project and project manager's quality

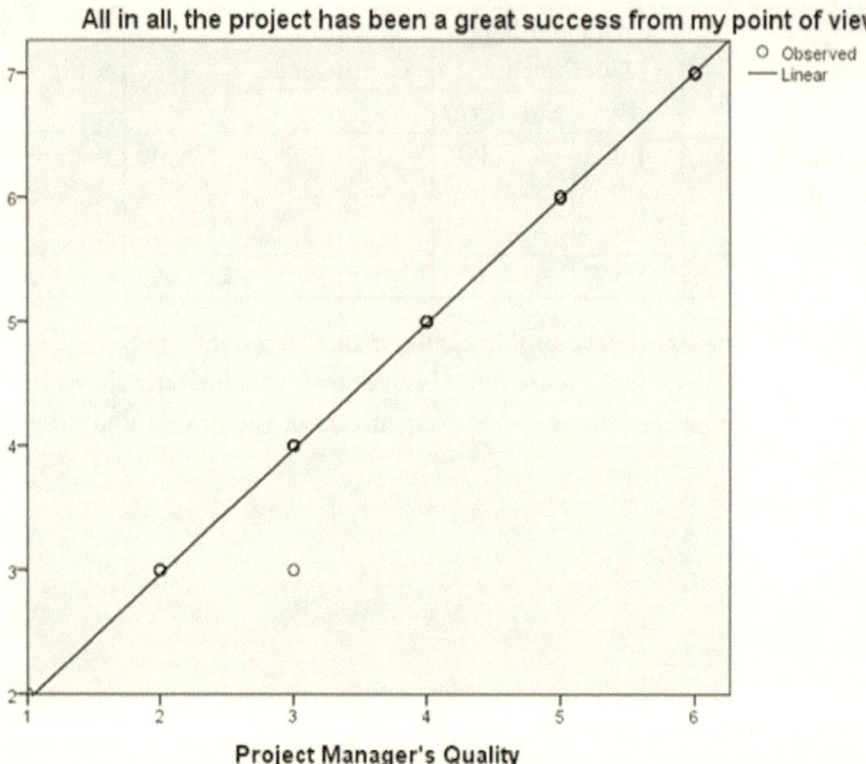

All in all, the project has been a great success from my point of view.

Project Manager's Quality

To confirm the relationship between the success of the project and project manager's quality a t-test have been performed and in the Table 3 shown below the p value is less than 0.05 therefore there exists a relationship between the success of the project and project manager's quality.

Table 3
Linear relationship between success of the
project and project manager's quality

	Unstandardized Coefficients		Standardized Coefficients		
	B	Std. Error	Beta	t	Sig.
Project Manager's Quality	1.012	.007	.997	154.714	.000
(Constant)	.938	.032		29.361	.000

To find the linear relationship between the success of the project and project planning and process efficiency Figure 9 has been drawn, which clearly shows that there exists a linear relationship between success of the project and project planning and process efficiency.

Figure 9
Linear relationship between success of the project
and project planning and process efficiency

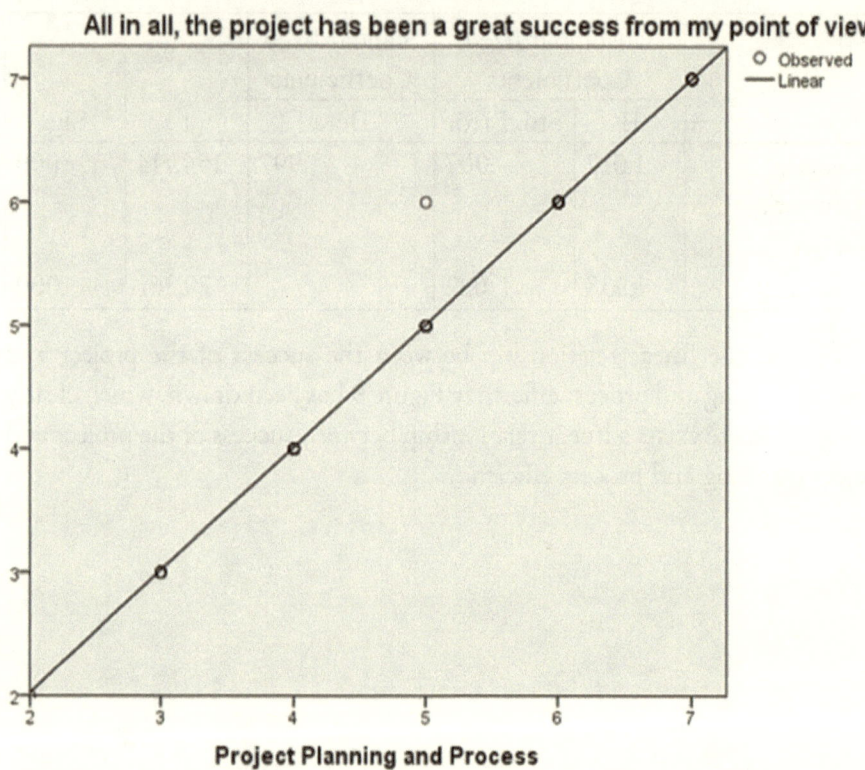

To confirm the relationship between the success of the project and project planning and process efficiency a t-test have been performed and in the Table 4 shown below the p value is less than 0.05 therefore there exists a relationship between the success of the project and project planning and process efficiency.

Table 4
Linear relationship between success of the project
and project planning and process efficiency

	Unstandardized Coefficients		Standardized Coefficients	t	Sig.
	B	Std. Error	Beta		
Project Planning and Process	.995	.006	.997	153.378	.000
(Constant)	.035	.038		.908	.365

To find the linear relationship between the success of the project and Communication with stakeholders Figure 10 has been drawn, which clearly shows that there exists a linear relationship between success of the project and Communication with stakeholders.

Figure 10
Linear relationship between success of the project
and Communication with stakeholders

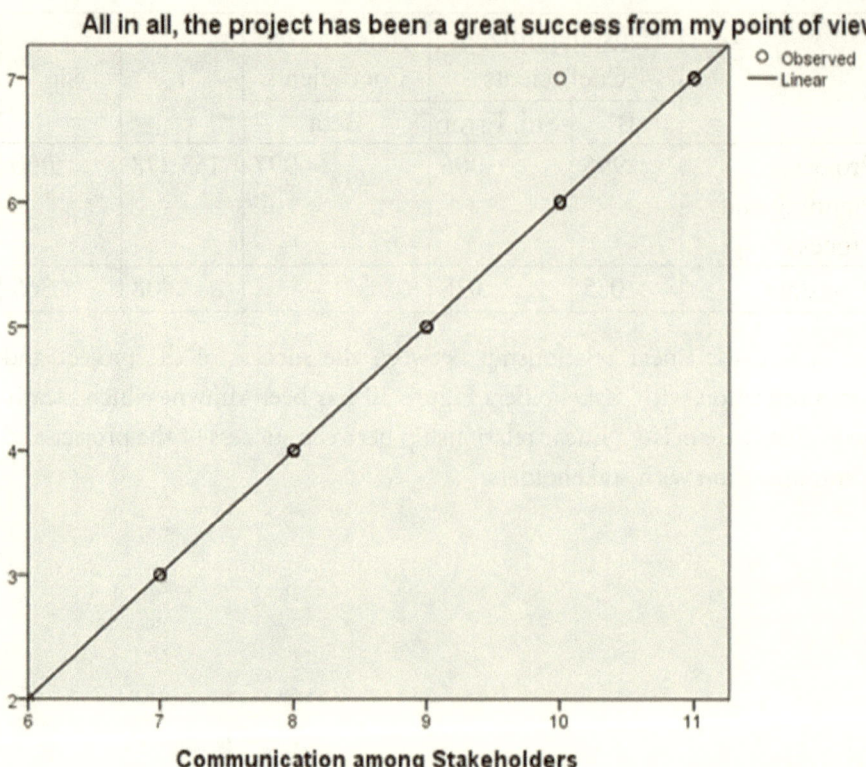

Communication among Stakeholders

To confirm the relationship between the success of the project and Communication with stakeholders a t-test have been performed and in the Table 5 shown below the p value is less than 0.05 therefore there exists a relationship between the success of the project and Communication with stakeholders.

Table 5
Linear relationship between success of the project
and Communication with stakeholders

	Unstandardized Coefficients		Standardized Coefficients	t	Sig.
	B	Std. Error	Beta		
Communication among Stakeholders	1.001	.007	.997	153.117	.000
(Constant)	-4.008	.064		-62.399	.000

To find the linear relationship between the success of the project and Technical best practices Figure 11 has been drawn, which clearly shows that there exists a linear relationship between success of the project and requirement analysis.

Figure 11
Linear relationship between success of the
project and requirement analysis

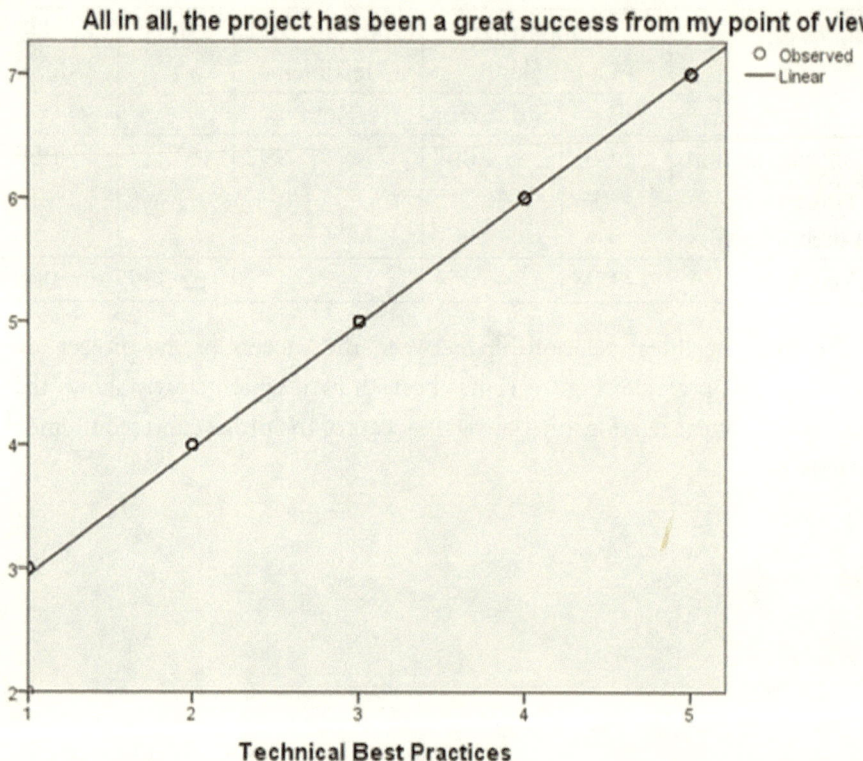

All in all, the project has been a great success from my point of view.

Technical Best Practices

To confirm the relationship between the success of the project and Technical best practices a t-test have been performed and in the Table 6 shown below the p value is less than 0.05 therefore there exists a relationship between the success of the project and Technical best practices.

Table 6
Linear relationship between success of the
project and requirement analysis

	Unstandardized Coefficients		Standardized Coefficients	t	Sig.
	B	Std. Error	Beta		
Technical Best Practices	1.018	.006	.997	157.198	.000
(Constant)	1.924	.025		75.935	.000

To find the linear relationship between the success of the project and testing Figure 12 has been drawn, which clearly shows that there exists a linear relationship between success of the project and Testing.

Figure 12
Linear relationship between success
of the project and testing

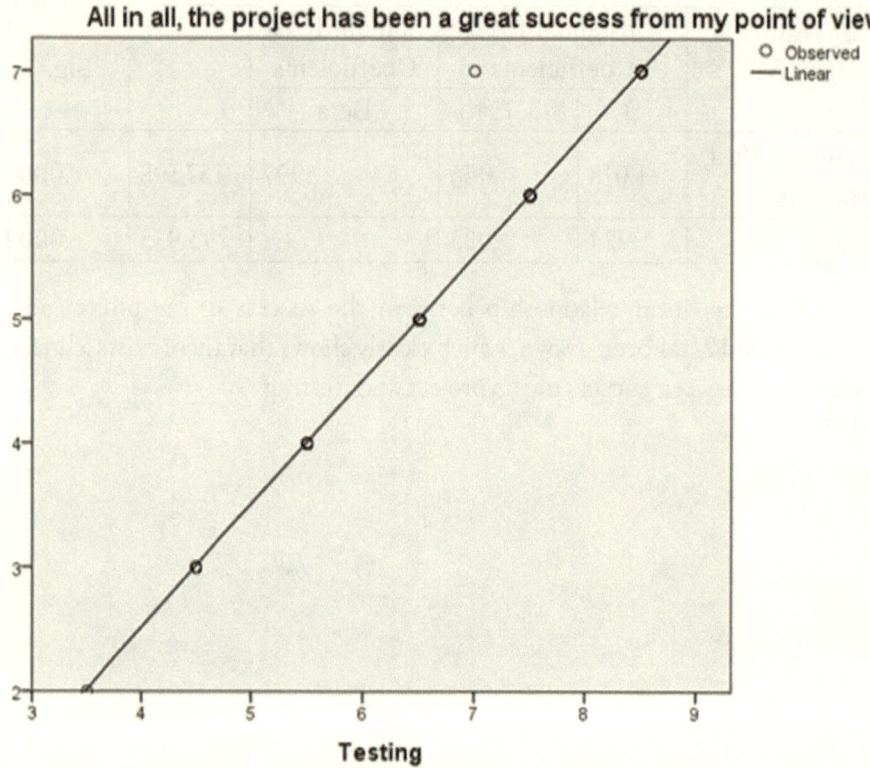

To confirm the relationship between the success of the project and Testing a t-test have been performed and in the Table 7 shown below the p value is less than 0.05 therefore there exists a relationship between the success of the project and testing.

Table 7
Linear relationship between success
of the project and testing

	Unstandardized Coefficients		Standardized Coefficients	t	Sig.
	B	Std. Error	Beta		
Testing	.997	.010	.993	101.680	.000
(Constant)	-1.472	.072		-20.453	.000

To find the linear relationship between the success of the project and client or user satisfaction Figure 13 has been drawn, which clearly shows that there exists a linear relationship between success of the project and client or user satisfaction.

Figure 13
Linear relationship between success of the
project and client/ user satisfaction

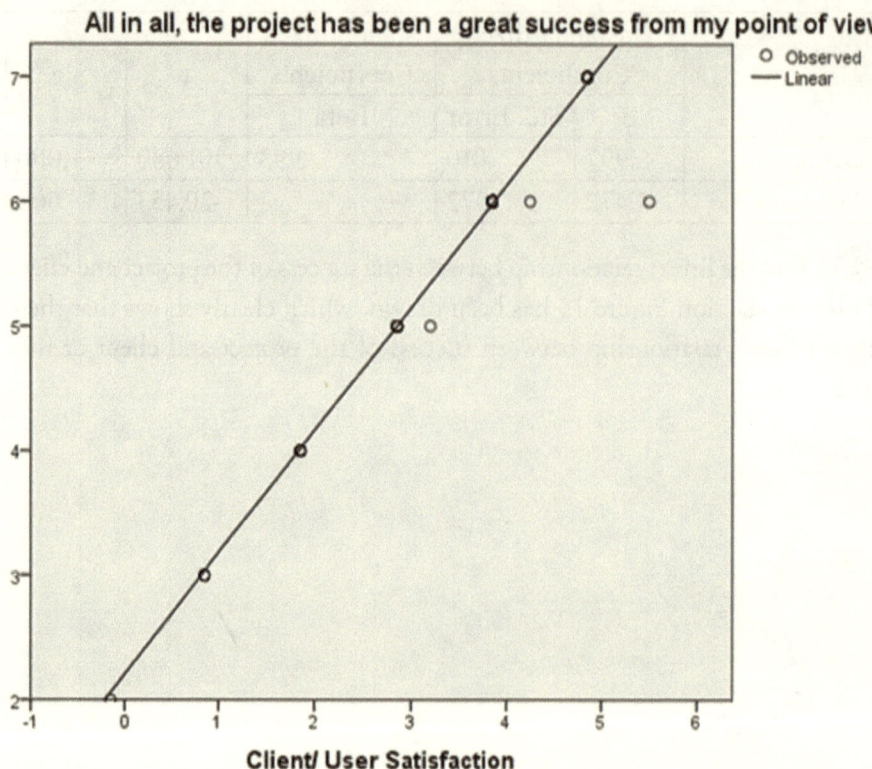

To confirm the relationship between the success of the project and client or user satisfaction a t-test have been performed and in the Table 8 shown below the p value is less than 0.05 therefore there exists a relationship between the success of the project and client or user satisfaction.

Table 8
Linear relationship between success of the project and client/ user satisfaction

	Unstandardized Coefficients		Standardized Coefficients	t	Sig.
	B	Std. Error	Beta		
Client or User Satisfaction	.980	.011	.991	88.978	.000
(Constant)	2.205	.042		52.880	.000

To find the linear relationship between the success of the project and Use of Automated tools in managing software projects Figure 14 has been drawn, which clearly shows that there exists a linear relationship between success of the project and use of automated tools in managing software projects.

Figure 14
Linear relationship between success of the
project and use of automated tools

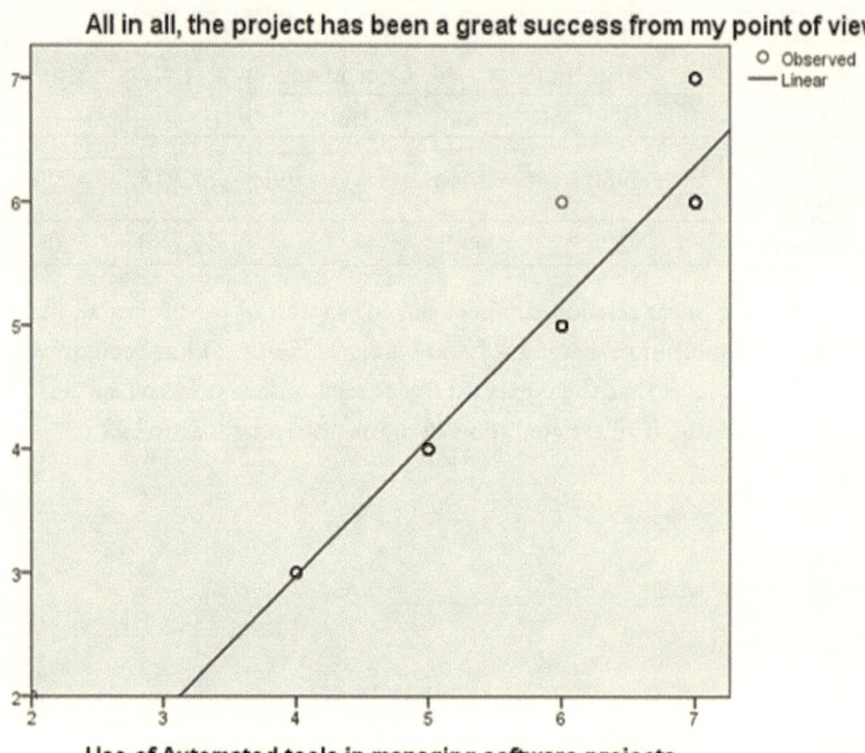

All in all, the project has been a great success from my point of view.

Use of Automated tools in managing software projects

To confirm the relationship between the success of the project and Use of Automated tools in managing software projects a t-test have been performed and in the Table 9 shown below the p value is less than 0.05 therefore there exists a relationship between the success of the project and Use of Automated tools in managing software projects.

Table 9
Linear relationship between success of the
project and use of automated tools

	Unstandardized Coefficients		Standardized Coefficients	t	Sig.
	B	Std. Error	Beta		
Use of Automated tools in managing software projects	1.107	.041	.912	27.045	.000
(Constant)	-1.453	.269		-5.393	.000

Once the linear relationship among each of the nine independent variables with the dependent variable is established, I have performed the linear regression. Table 10 given below show that, all the independent variables have significant relationship with the Success of the project.

Dr. Tuhin Chattopadhyay

Table 10
Multiple Regression Coefficients

Model	Unstandardized Coefficients		Standardized Coefficients	t	Sig.
	B	Std. Error	Beta		
(Constant)	.397	.156		2.542	.012
Project Manager's Quality	.162	.027	.160	5.958	.000
Project Planning and Process	.125	.027	.125	4.569	.000
Technical Best Practices	.095	.042	.093	2.293	.023
Use of Automated tools in managing software projects	.024	.008	.020	3.174	.002
Communication among Stakeholders	.117	.028	.117	4.231	.000
Clarity of understanding of Requirement / Feasibility analysis of requirement	.240	.036	.240	6.630	.000
Testing	.052	.019	.052	2.717	.007
Team Members' Quality	.166	.045	.162	3.702	.000
Client/ User Satisfaction	.036	.017	.036	2.159	.033

From the last column of table 10, I find that all the p values of the corresponding independent variables are less that 0.05, thusIhave got sufficient evidence to conclude that all the independent variables are individually leaving

84

an impact on the success of the project. To test whether all the independent variables collectively leave an influence on the success of the projectIperform an ANOVA as exhibited in Table 11

Table 11
ANOVA

Model		Sum of Squares	Df	Mean Square	F	Sig.
1	Regression	158.175	9	17.575	20851.843	.000
	Residual	.118	140	.001		
	Total	158.293	149			

Table 11, with p value less than .05, provides evidence that the model as a whole is significant.

The model summary presented in Table 12 shows the predictability power of our model. The value of adjusted R^2 is 99.9% which means that all our independent variables taken together can explain 99.9% of variation in the success of the project.

Table12
Model Summary

R	R Square	Adjusted R Square	Std. Error of the Estimate
1.000	.999	.999	.029

Once it has been found that all the independent variables collectively explain almost the entire variation of the success of the project, the model is provided below:

Success of the project = .397 + 0.240 Clarity of understanding of Requirement/ Feasibility analysis + 0.166 Team member's quality + 0.162 Project manager's quality + 0.125 Project Planning and process efficiency + 0.117 Communication with stakeholders + 0.095 Technical best practices + 0.052 Testing + 0.036 Client/ user satisfaction + 0.024 Use of Automated tools in managing software projects

From the equation it can be interpreted that clarity of understanding of requirement or feasibility analysis leaves the highest impact on the success of the project with its coefficient as 0.24; team member's quality leaves the second highest impact on the success of the project with its coefficient as 0.167; project manager's quality leaves the third highest impact with its coefficient as 0.162; project planning and process efficiency leaves the fourth highest impact with its coefficient as 0.125; communication with stakeholders leaves the fifth highest impact with its coefficient as 0.117; technical best practices leaves the sixth highest impact with its coefficient as 0.93; testing leaves the seventh highest impact with its coefficient as 0.052; client/ user satisfaction leaves the eighth highest impact with its coefficient as 0.036 and use of automated tools in managing software projects leaves the least impact with its coefficient as 0.02. Thus the required equation helps us to figure out the impact factor of the success of the software project in order of their importance.

Chapter 14

Discussion and Conclusion

In all the previous chapters, I have tried to bring out the most important aspects of software development project. The empirical study in the result chapter helps us in validating the same. As discussed a project is a set of distinct activities grouped together with the aim of attaining a specified goal, which is equally applicable to software projects. In the present scenario, where globalization is influencing everything, the projects too are happening at global level. The software project management focuses on four P's: People, Product, Process and Project. The success of the software projects is traditionally evaluated on three core parameters; timeliness, budget conformance and the one which deliverers all agreed upon functionality. Development of software has always been a tricky process and as compared to other engineering projects it is more complex and non consistent, where the nature of end product is intangible. But on an average the software's that are developed are not able to satisfy above criterion.

Before starting the software development processes its essential to establish the feasibility of the proposal. The most important step is to do the feasibility analysis; functional and monetary. At the end of this stage scope of the proposed project is define clearly the estimates of the project are given. It is during this phase that any project is given green signal. Thus the business problem in various functional areas begins it journey to get solved through automation of the business process. Any mistake at this point leads to high failure rate as the incorrect beginning definitely ends up into a disaster. The regression result shows that the coefficient for clarity of understanding of requirement or feasibility analysis of requirement is 0.024 which is highest of all the variables in the study. This is in accordance with the fact that technical, functional, legal and economic feasibility analysis can only drive a successful software project. This step also takes into consideration initial inputs by the customer which further reduces the chances of futile efforts during the course of the project.

It is said that technology is created by human beings and hence it cannot surpass them in every aspect. The project involves team members coming from different skill set together to achieve a particular objective and then it disperses. Globalization and outsourcing of software projects further add to the dynamic nature of the project teams. Thus to get good work done it's important to hire right people with the right skill set. Apart from the different type of the task each set of project team members perform, the diversity is also introduced among them on account of different culture and time zones. The ability of the team members to perform well and as single unit with understanding the common objective and overcoming the conflicts is extremely important for good results in a software project. The same is validated by the coefficient of Team Members' Quality in the regression table being second highest i.e. 0.166 among the nine variables. Transparent and clear communication is a major challenge in project teams, which further lead issues like, lack of trust, team conflict and inability to make proper decisions within time. Thus it is vital to have team members with qualities which enable them to perform better inspite of these complexities.

A project manager is at the centre of all the activities in a software development project. He also acts as bridge between the business needs and its corresponding technical representation. Inspite of efficient team members, a team constantly requires proper guidance and a direction which make them work as per the big picture in the project. The project manager is also required to provide clarity about role of individuals in the team while managing the expectations of senior executives and the team members. A project manager plays a pivotal role in a software project, being involved right from the planning and definition of the scope to the closure of the project. Apart from managing the project a project manager must also exhibit appropriate leadership quality.

The next highest coefficient in the result reflects this importance of project manager's quality i.e. 0.162. The desired qualities in a project manager may be inbuilt or may acquire trough proper training. Accurate planning of a software project, including proper sequencing and integration of essential elements of development process is very important for project success. After putting the team together an effective plan should be executed and it is very much obvious from the empirical result where the coefficient of Project Planning and Process is 0.125.

Like all the projects even in the software development projects involves different stakeholders. A software project is declared failed when the end product i.e. the software, does not meet the requirements specified by the customers at the beginning or if there is cost and time overrun. The nonconformance to the required functionality is mostly due to lack of stakeholder involvement and poor stakeholder management. A good project manager realizes that involvement of stakeholders in the various phases of software development contribute in the quality software product. Identification and communication with all the stakeholders is critical for the software project. The importance of effective and transparent communication with stakeholders is supported by the respective coefficient which is 0.117. Thus all the stakeholders' acquirers, assessors, communicators, developers, maintainers, production engineers, suppliers, support staff, system administrators, testers and customers should be equally taken care of.

Software development has an interesting angle to it; software development process leads to technological advancements and itself is technology driven. The success of a software project is dependent upon the right choice of technology, tools and methodology adopted to carry out the project. Technical best practices provide a guideline to get good results in the software development project. From the result, I get enough evidence regarding the importance of following Technical Best Practices, with coefficient as 0.093. Thus a project manager must focus in selecting appropriate development methodology, suitable software architecture and design, doing software project risk analysis and making use of use of software specialists.

Good quality of the product is a key to customer satisfaction and software products are no exception. Software failure is a major concern for the software development organizations. Software development organizations are focusing on process improvement and TQM for enhanced software quality and productivity of the development firm. Quality has become one of the key to software success as well as the key market factor for high technology. Software quality comes from good testing plan and methodologies. Software development firms need to allocate appropriate budget for the same. Software testing, can be define that as a process of executing a program with the goal of finding errors. A strategy for bug fixing involving offline and online strategies must be employed. Along with the use of effective test cases automated testing should also be used. Significance of testing is well supported by the regression table where the corresponding coefficient is 0.052.

The success of the project largely depends upon the satisfaction of the users and customers. Like all businesses the success of IT sector also needs to focus on enhancing customer satisfaction in the delivery of services and products. With respect to software products achieving satisfied customers is much more difficult, as it depends upon how effectively the development process delivers the final product as desired by the customers. The project manager needs to focus on these factors to create more satisfied customer. Thus a deep understanding of ways to keep the project on track so that it complies with the definition of the software project is critical. There are two very important activities which help in doing so; estimation and developing baseline budget for project. One of the most important stakeholders in the software projects are customers and their satisfaction signifies the success of the software project with regression coefficient as 0.036 For project managers it is very important that the cost estimation is being done very accurately, to make a software project successful. When a project fulfills all the promised functionality with estimated budget and time, customer is highly satisfied and a satisfied customer has enormous contribution in the success of the software project. Lot of effort goes into making a software project successful; right from appropriate requirement gathering, studying the feasibility, planning effectively, managing the risk and proper maintenance of the software product. Thus the last but not the least important factor to be taken care of is making use of automated software project management tools, with regression coefficient equal to 0.020. If all these factors are managed by a project manager properly, a software project is bound to be a successful one. Thus all the project managers who are having hard time dealing with various aspects of the software development process are sure to be benefitted with the factually and empirically supported recipe for a project with higher probability of success.

References

Ambriola, V. & Genoveffa, T. (1993). Advances in Software Engineering and Knowledge Engineering. World Scientific.

Bass, L. Clements, P. and Kazman, R.(2003). Software Architecture in Practice.

Boehm, B. (1989). Software Risk Management. Washington, DC, IEEE Computer Society Press.

Burns, M. (2008). Project management to the rescue. CA Magazine; Mar; 141, 2; ABI/INFORM Global, pg. 22.

Cleland, D. (1998). Field Guide to Project management. ISBN-10: 0442023456 | ISBN-13: 9780442023454

Csikszentmihalyi, Mihaly (1975). Beyond Boredom and Anxiety: The Experience of Play in Work and Games. San Francisco: Jossey-Bass, Inc.

Gobeli, D. H., Koenig, H. F., & Bechinger, I. (1998). Managing conflict in software development teams: A multilevel analysis. Journal of Product Innovation Management, 15, 423-435.

Honold, L. (1997). A review of the literature on employee empowerment. Empowerment in Organizations, Vol. 5 Iss: 4 pp. 202 – 212

Haughey, D. (2012). Project planning a Step by Step Guide, retrieved on 9th Dec 2012, from http://www.projectsmart.co.uk/project-planning-step-by-step.html.

Henri Fayol's (1916). General and Industrial Management.

IBM survey (2008). "The IBM Global making change work study". Retrieved from: ftp://public.dhe.ibm.com/common/ssi/ecm/en/.../GBE03100USEN. PDF

Krigsman, M. (2010). Shocking gov't IT failure statistics. Retrieved from http://www.zdnet.com/blog/projectfailures/...govt-it-failure-statistics/10490

Kujala, S. et al. (2005). The Role of User Involvement in Requirement Quality and Project Success. Proceedings of the 2005 13th IEEE International Conference on Requirement Engineering, Paris, France, Aug 29 – Sept 2, 2005

Mabert, V.M., Soni, A. and Venkataramanan, M.A. (2000), "Enterprise resource planning survey of US manufacturing firms", Production and Inventory Management Journal, Vol. 41 No. 2, pp. 52-88.

Mallak, L.A. and Kurstedt, H.A., Jr.,. (1996), "Understanding and using empowerment to change organizational culture," Industrial Management, November/December, pp. 8-10.

McManus, J. & Wood-Harper, T. (2005). The British Computer Society EDIT study of projects in the European Union by REFRAME (Business LINE/ APA). Retrieved from: http://www.bcs.org/content/ConWebDoc/19584(2008).

McEachern, C. (2005). A Look Inside Offshoring: Customers are Less Satisfied with Offshore Service Providers. VARBusiness. Retrieved from www.varbusiness.com/article/showArticle.jhtml?articleId=166403041

Mekikian, G. and Roberts, J. (2009). Tata Consultancy Services, Globalization of IT Services. Stanford Case Studies. Retrieved from www.tcs.com/about/corp_facts/Pages/default.aspx

Mike Wooldridge (2000) President and CEO, retrieved from www.cs.ox.ac.uk/people/michael.wooldridge/teaching/soft-eng/

Moore, D. (1999). The hoover dam:A world renowned concrete monument. Retrieved from http://www.romanconcrete.com/HooverDam.htm.

Moore, C. (2003). Project tools unite, InfoWorld; Jul 28, 25, 29; ABI/INFORM Global, pg. 18.

Moran, D. (2009). The Elusive Definition of Success with Software Projects. November 27. Retrieved from: http://www.softwareresults.us/2009/11/elusive-definition-of-success-with.html.

Nasir, Mohd H. N. & Sahibuddin, S. (2011). Critical success factors for software projects: A comparative study. Scientific Research and Essays Vol. 6(10), pp. 2174-2186, 18 May. Available online at http://www.academicjournals.org/SRE ISSN 1992-2248 ©2011 Academic Journals.

Nokes, S. (2007). The Definitive Guide to Project Management.. 2nd Ed.n. London (Financial Times / Prentice Hall): ISBN 978-0-273-71097-4.

Prinzo R. (2011). Five Challenges to Software Implementation and How to Avoid Them (and Realize Real ROI as a Result) ....Retrieved from www.teamsoftware.com/solutions-and.../WhitePaper-Implementation.pdf

Project Management Institute (U.S.). A guide to the project management body of knowledge (PMBOK® Guide), 4th ed.

Quinn, L. S. (2010). Six Views of Project Management Software. Retrieved from: http://idealware.org/articles/six-views-project-management-software-0, Founder and Executive Director of Idealware.

Reel, J. S. (1999). "Critical success factors in software projects," IEEE Software, pp. 18–23.

Riley, R. (2006), "7 Tips for a Successful Software Project – CodeProject" retrieved from, www.codeproject.com › ... › Work Issues › General

Ron P. (2001). Software Testing. Retrieved from http://books.google.co.in/books/about/Software_testing.html?

Sauer C and Cuthbertson C (2003). The State of IT Project Management in the UK 2002-2003. Computer Weekly, 15 April, pp. 1-8

Shaw and Garlan (1996). Software Architecture, Perspectives on an Emerging Discipline, Prentice-Hall.

Swebok (2004). The Guide to the Software Engineering Body of Knowledge (SWEBOK)

Snyder, James R. and Kline, Smith. (March, 1987) "Modern Project Management: How DidIGet Here – Where DoIGo?" Project Management Journal.

Wideman, M. (2002). Wideman comparative glossary of common management terms V3.1.

Wateridge, J. (1997). "How can is/it projects be measured for success?" International Journal of Project Management, vol. 16, no. 1, pp. 59–63

Zwikael, O. (2008), "Top management involvement in project management – exclusive support practices for different project scenarios", International Journal of Managing Projects in Business, Vol. 1 No. 3.

www.ingramcontent.com/pod-product-compliance
Lightning Source LLC
Chambersburg PA
CBHW022107170526
45157CB00004B/1527